In THE P.L.O. CONNECTIONS, Dr. John Laffin considers
many aspects of this blood-chilling enigma of our times,
including:

* The rise of the P.L.O. and its aims
* Leadership
* Propaganda
* Finance
* The Soviet Connection
* Support for Amin and Khomeini
* Schools for Terrorism

THE P.L.O. CONNECTIONS

JOHN LAFFIN

CORGI BOOKS
A DIVISION OF TRANSWORLD PUBLISHERS LTD

THE P.L.O. CONNECTIONS
A CORGI BOOK 0 552 12090 1

First publication in Great Britain

PRINTING HISTORY

Corgi edition published 1982

Copyright © John Laffin 1982

This book is set in 10 pt. Plantin

Corgi Books are published by Transworld Publishers Ltd.,
Century House, 61-63 Uxbridge Road, Ealing, London W5 5SA

Made and printed in Great Britain by
Hunt Barnard Printing Ltd., Aylesbury, Bucks.

Contents

Chapter One

The Many Faces of the PLO

Episodes and interviews are the stock-in-trade of a writer who works more in the field than in his study. And when they are intense experiences they can be more revealing and informative than any amount of studious research. Most of the following episodes directly involved me as observer-on-the spot, some have been reported by other professionals. All show various aspects of the Palestine Liberation Organisation and they are presented here with only little comment. Analysis is not necessary.

Yasser Arafat and the chicken

Through a Palestinian working for the United Nations Relief and Works Agency, I met Yasser Arafat (code-name Abu Ammar), chairman of the PLO, in the summer of 1973 and talked with him at some length in the offices of the PLO's "Research" Institute in Beirut. The massacre of the Israeli athletes at Munich had taken place only a year before and I told Arafat that I was interested in the type of indoctrination which could induce young men to carry out such a ruthless and bloody act.

'So you are interested,' Arafat said with a throaty chuckle. 'Well, I will personally show you how we train our boys.'

He made a telephone call and later I accompanied him in a chauffeur-driven car to a refugee camp at Ein el Hilwe in southern Lebanon. With us was a bodyguard of half a dozen heavily armed terrorists, the UNRWA official and a PLO press officer. These two made some murmured excuse and left us at the entrance to the camp, where Arafat was greeted with great respect and delight.

Deep inside the camp we reached a military training area, with a sub-machine-gun firing range and various obstacles for an assault course. As we arrived about eighty boys aged from eight to fourteen, dressed in camouflage training uniforms, were hard at work under shouting instructors. Some were running along a ramp and then leaping through a smoky fire. They too were shouting.

At this point it all looked rather like energetic boy scout or young cadet training. Arafat frequently applauded and called compliments to the boys and their instructors, though they could have heard little of what he said through their own chanting. A large basket was brought and the boys were put into a semi-circle around it. An instructor gave an order and a boy reached into the basket and pulled out a struggling chicken.

Then, with brisk efficiency, he wrung its neck and dropped the dead bird.

'No, no, no!' Arafat said reprovingly. He too reached into the basket and dragged out a chicken. And without wringing its neck he pulled the thing apart. After a few minutes he threw down the dismembered bird and somebody handed him a towel to wipe the blood from his hands. 'So!' he said in a tone which meant, 'That's how it's done.' We waited while a couple of boys carried out a similar ritual, which is best not fully described here.

Arafat turned to me and said again, 'So—this is how we teach the boys to deal with the Isra-eelis.' He looked really pleased with himself. I have seen much bloodshed over many years but that blood on Arafat's hands sickened me more than most.

The next time I saw those hands they were being held high in triumph before the braying applause of the United Nations Assembly.

* * *

The Broken Wing

In January 1972 the Arab Palestinian artist I. Shammout, then working for the PLO Cultural Arts Section in Beirut, presented me with two greetings cards which he had illustrated. I have them still—'To John Laffin with my compliments.'

One is entitled *The Broken Wing* and it shows an elderly Arab woman, another woman of about 30 and a small child; they are seated in a group before what appears to be a border fence and a wrecked house. The younger woman is holding a wounded white dove to her breast while in the background is the figure of a man who seems, from the expression on the woman's face, to have shot the bird.

The other card is entitled *Persistence*. The drawing is mostly taken up with a woman in an embroidered jacket busily mending an article of clothing. She has sensitive, rather sad eyes as she bends to her work. In the background two young men are studying by lantern light at a table.

The cards, an indirect and moving plea for sympathy for homeless refugees, were being sold in Beirut to help raise funds for the PLO cause.

Mr. Shammout, a quietly spoken and gentle man, told me that he had found great inspiration in being a refugee. 'There is no art without suffering,' he said.

* * *

'If we have to kill Jews. . . .'

Ghassan Kanafani, a sensitive novelist and a bitter revolutionary—an interesting blend of genuine intellectual and man of action—was, until mid-1972, spokesman for George Habash's terrorist group, Popular Front for the Liberation of Palestine. Aged 35, Kanafani, with whom I talked at length several times, said, 'The relentless march of history is more important than immediate events of any kind.' The previous September in a bloody war—'Black September'—King Hussein had driven the PLO out of

Jordan. Kanafani thought that Arafat and his personal part of the PLO, Fatah, were being too sentimental about this reverse. 'Our revolution is only in its pre-revolution phase,' he said. 'The anti-Zionist part is unimportant; it is only the catalyst for the Arab revolution. What we are aiming for is an all-Arab social and cultural revolution. If we have to kill Jews to bring it about then we will kill Jews. People are too stupidly sentimental about life.'

It was Kanafani who publicly announced PFLP's part in the Tel Aviv Airport massacre in which 24 Christian pilgrims to Israel were killed and another 66, mostly Puerto Ricans, were wounded.

Kanafani got into his car, with his niece, outside his home in Beirut on July 8, 1972 and as he started the engine a booby-trap blew him to pieces. At the time a BBC correspondent in Beirut reported that a PFLP splinter group could have been responsible. Naturally, PLO propaganda blamed the Israelis. Because Kanafani had publicly announced the PFLP's part in the airport massacre some Palestinians believed that the Israelis had killed him in revenge. I have heard six or seven different groups blamed for Kanafani's death and no doubt as many as this had their own reasons for wanting him dead.

* * *

The Hijacking Class

One night in April 1974 a PLO woman official I had met in Beirut called for me at my hotel, the Alcazar, and asked me to come immediately as she had 'something interesting' to show me. I was blindfolded in her car which was then driven around aimlessly for about half an hour to confuse my sense of direction. The woman and her two men companions were very apologetic about the need for this but, they told me, it was necessary for security. Changes of gear told me we were climbing into the hills.

When we pulled up and the blindfold was removed I saw that we were in a courtyard with high walls. Inside a building the woman, with the air of a compère at a command performance, showed me rooms full of weapons, ammunition, explosives and grenades. I recognised Russian, American, Czech and British-made material—all of it new and expensive.

'As you see we are prepared for anything,' the woman said. I had never doubted it but the display was impressive.

'How well can you use all this stuff?' I said.

'Well enough,' one of the men said and with brisk efficiency he stripped some of the weapons and reassembled them.

The woman said that next day she would show me something even more interesting. This time I was taken without blindfold to a PLO refugee camp with terrorist training facilities which I did not know until later was Baddawi, near Tripoli. Here, to my real surprise, I saw two full-size mock-ups of a Boeing 707 and a Boeing 747. Grouped nearby were about 80 people, some of them decidedly more European and Latin-American in appearance than Arab.

Slightly apart from the main group were two women of European appearance, also in a form of uniform. A man wearing a quasi-military uniform was lecturing the large group, in English, through a loud hailer. And he was telling them about hijacking techniques; as I listened he was making a point about the necessity to have all aircraft doors in sight to prevent hostages from escaping and to meet any attempt to rush the plane.

My guide had disappeared but she now came back, flushed and uncomfortable, in the middle of a posse of men who surrounded me and insistently but politely enough hustled me away. It was clear that the woman was in a lot of trouble for having brought me there and she sat in sullen silence on the way back to Beirut.

Baddawi was run by George Habash's branch of the PLO, the Popular Front for the Liberation of Palestine. I heard later that the Boeing mock-ups were still in use in December 1975 and that on December 2 of that year the Israeli Air Force bombed them.

* * *

A Sniper's Target

On October 9, 1975, a Chicago photographer, Mike Schiff, arrived in Beirut on an assignment from Robert Fenton, director of *Faces* Magazine, to get pictures of the PLO in action during the Lebanese war. He was readily accepted by the PLO as are most journalists and photographers who profess sympathy for the organisation's cause. A few days later he was present at a PLO post when a radio broadcast announced yet another truce and cease-fire.

The post commander at once selected three youthful members of Fatah, the PLO's military wing, and ordered them into the streets. 'Make damn sure that the city does *not* get back to normal,' he told them.

Schiff accompanied them on their patrol. With AK-47 or assault rifles slung over their shoulders the PLO men climbed to the roof of a three-storey building. Here they positioned themselves with a clear view of a bread line forming below them. These people of Beirut had also heard about the cease-fire and were taking advantage of it to get food; from experience they knew the lull would not last long. A woman, clutching a small child to her breast, was crossing the street. 'Watch this,' the youngest of the trio said to Schiff. He fired two shots. The woman and child crumpled into a pile of rags in the road.*

* * *

The Refrigerator Killer

During 1980-81 producer Barbara Newman and correspondent Geraldo Rivera of the US television programme ABC News spent eight months working on a programme about the PLO. Several terrorists spoke candidly of their training in the Soviet Union and of their desire to destroy Israel, even if it meant killing every Jew in the country.

One exchange is particularly interesting. Rivera spoke

* Schiff's story is told in *Soldier of Fortune*, Winter 1977.

to a terrorist who had planted a bomb in a refrigerator in Zion Square, Jerusalem, killing 15 passersby and wounding 87.

Question: So you killed Israelis?
Answer: Oh yes, because they took my land.
Question: Women, children?
Answer: Women, children, I don't care.
Question: But the Israeli women and children, were they your enemy?
Answer: Everyone who lives in my home is my enemy.
Question: And you will kill them?
Answer: Oh yes.
Question: Even the children?
Answer: Even . . . anybody. Those children, after 10 or 15 years, is being a man, and he is a soldier, and the Israelis make him a soldier. Right or not?
Question: So you are proud of the fact that you killed these people?
Answer: Oh sure, oh sure.
Question: And your conscience is clear?
Answer: Oh yes, this is my own business.

* * *

The Child Hostages
In the early hours of April 7, 1980 several small Israeli children, aged six months to three years, were asleep in the children's house of Kibbutz Misgav Am, not far from Israel's northern border. Five terrorists from the Arab Liberation Front infiltrated through the area controlled by the United Nations peace-keeping force and took the children hostage in the house. They demanded that 50 convicted comrades be released from Israeli prisons; if not the children would be killed.

Various negotiations were tried, including one by Sami Shani, the 35-year-old secretary of the kibbutz. The terrorists shot him dead. They also killed Eyal Gluska, aged two and a half. Just before the expiry of the terrorists' deadline Israeli soldiers stormed the building and killed the terrorists, though four children were hurt.

The ALF is an Iraqi-based group operating from Lebanon under the overall control of the PLO. Its leader, 'Abd ar-Rahim Ahmad, is a key member of the PLO executive and a strong supporter of Yasser Arafat. The attack could not have been carried out without the knowledge and approval of the PLO executive and possibly of Arafat himself, who the day before had addressed an ALF meeting in Beirut.

On April 12 the children's supplement of Iraq's official daily newspaper, *A–Thawra*, published a poem glorifying the episode as an heroic military exploit.

* * *

A Woman's Work

Mrs. Umm Khalaf, now 40, was the first girl to join Fatah—at the age of 16. The struggle to preserve a Palestinian identity at the time was so strong, she says, that 'a Palestinian woman had to do a man's work'. She did this work to such effect that she became a marksman with the automatic rifle she still carries in her car in Beirut. She can also handle an anti-tank gun.

As the wife of one of the PLO's leaders, 'Abu Iyad', Mrs. Khalaf has a lot of responsibilities. She is head of the General Union of Palestinian Women, an organisation that claims 100,000 members and which supports many of the PLO's programmes in health and education. She also directs the PLO's multi-million-pound assistance programme for families of Palestinians killed or captured in conflicts with the Israelis, Lebanese and Jordanians.

She grew up in Gaza and in that vast Egyptian slum, as it was then, she became an ardent nationalist. She is, in a sense, jealous of the Israelis' success in making the land of ancient Palestine prosperous.

Mrs. Khalaf and her husband named the first of their four children, a son, Jihad (Arabic for "holy war") though she tells foreign journalists, 'We are looking for peace, not war. But we are fighting for our rights in order to provide our children with a normal life.'

She lives with the knowledge that her husband could be assassinated at any time in a PLO factional intrigue. If he were to be wounded he would be well treated at one of the 35 hospitals operated by the PLO. Mrs. Khalaf's work brings her into contact with Dr. Fathi Arafat, younger brother of Yasser, and chairman of the Palestinian Red Crescent Organisation. He has been in charge of the PLO medical and social programme since 1965.

Both Mrs. Khalaf and Dr. Arafat deplore Western ignorance of the PLO's humanitarian work and when Western journalists say to them, 'But as your propaganda is almost entirely political what can you expect?' they make an enigmatic hand gesture and do not answer.

* * *

The Vatican Connection

On the afternoon of March 18, 1981 a black car with a Vatican number plate swept through St. Anne's Gate of the Vatican and took the VIP route straight on through three tiny courtyards—Court of the Little Sentinel, Borgia Court and Parrots' Court. The personage in the car was conducted to a larger courtyard, Saint Damasus Court, the heart of the Apostolic Palace traffic. Saint Damasus Court is very much off the tourist beat but on this afternoon the visitor was anything but a tourist.

He was Farouk Khaddoumi, chief of the PLO's political department, sometimes described as its Foreign Minister. He was received by Cardinal Agostino Casaroli, the Vatican's Secretary-General and second only to the Pope in the Vatican hierarchy. For Khaddoumi to be received by Cardinal Casaroli, in the Vatican, was a pinnacle of PLO achievement.

Khaddoumi, whose PLO code-name is Abu Lutf, had the advantage of a friend at court—Greek Archbishop Hilarian Capucci. Capucci had been a gun-runner, convicted in 1974 of smuggling arms to terrorist organisations on the West Bank, and sentenced to 12 years in prison.

After repeated requests from the Vatican, the Israelis released him in 1977, on a Vatican promise that he would refrain from activity in Middle East politics. In fact, before he arranged for Khaddoumi's visit to the Vatican he had been to Damascus and Beirut and later he helped to promote the Iranian revolution of Ayatollah Khomeini.

The Khaddoumi audience was a testimony to the effectiveness of years of PLO propaganda. In Beirut, Arafat is said to have been received by Pope Paul Vl in May 1974 but the Vatican denies this.

* * *

Chapter Two

The Phenomenon

The Palestine Liberation Organisation officially came into being on May 22, 1964 and became the pioneer of modern terrorism. Its various groups were bent on the destruction of Israel as a state and the Israelis as a people —and of anybody else who got in the way of this design.

PLO members have carried out many hundreds of violent attacks—hijackings, bombings, kidnappings, massacres and individual murders. They deny few of these crimes. The PLO became, during the 1970s, the pivot of international terrorism in training, finance and inspiration and involved itself in terrorism in most countries. Palestinians have had active links with the Irish Republican Army, Baader-Meinhof, Red Army Faction, Japanese Red Army, and stores of other dissident groups with a history of violence in their own countries and across their borders.

The PLO has been a great destabilising force of the larger Middle East, plotting and carrying out assassinations, attempted assassinations, coups and subversion in Turkey, Lebanon, Jordan, Saudi Arabia, Egypt, Sudan, Iran, Morocco, Iraq, Sudan and Tunisia.

Within the PLO scores of murders have been committed as leaders of rival factions have schemed for control. Some of the constituent groups—or cells within groups —have achieved notoriety as hit squads of singular skill. Palestinian assassins have been responsible for murders in London, Paris, Antwerp, Athens, Amsterdam, Madrid,

Washington, Lisbon, Munich, Istanbul, Rome, Nicosia, and in many Arab cities.

For terrorism, political activism, publicity and propaganda on such a vast scale great amounts of money are needed. The PLO's money has come not only from grants by the Arab oil states but from trafficking in drugs, from blackmail, extortion and theft—as well as from legitimate investment in Western enterprise.

Terrorism has become commonplace in many parts of the world since the PLO established it as a fact of modern political life. But the Palestinian groups still hold various records in the field of terrorism. They include:

The largest hijacking. September 1970, Popular Front for the Liberation of Palestine (PFLP) hijacked four aircraft in a single operation. A Pan American plane was blown up at Cairo while Swissair, BOAC and TWA aircraft were destroyed near Amman. A fifth plane, from El Al, evaded hijack.

The largest number of hostages held at one time. Following the multiple hijack 300 passengers were held hostage for political blackmail—the release of terrorists held by Britain, Switzerland and Germany. The blackmail was successful.

The largest number of victims killed and wounded by a single booby-trap bomb. July 4, 1975. Fifteen Israelis were killed and 87 wounded by a PLO bomb planted in a refrigerator in Zion Square, Jerusalem.

The largest number of casualties in a terrorist raid. March 11, 1978. Fatah terrorists killed 38 people and wounded 70 after seizing two buses of Israelis on a holiday outing. The operation was approved by Yasser Arafat.

The worst mid-air explosion. February 21, 1970. A Swiss airliner blew up and 38 passengers and 9 crew members were killed. The PFLP General Command claimed responsibility.

The largest number of people shot at an airport. December 17, 1973. Black September killed 31 people at Rome airport; 29 were aboard a Pan Am plane.

The most sustained terrorist campaign. Between September 1967 and December 1980 terrorists affiliated with the PLO carried out at least 300 attacks—bombings, shootings, hijackings, rocket attacks, kidnappings—in 26 countries. Total casualties: 813 killed, 1013 injured. More than 90 per cent of the 2755 hostages were not Israelis.

The largest ransoms. In February 1972 PFLP hijacked a Lufthansa aircraft to Aden and held the passengers to ransom for five million dollars, which Lufthansa paid. In October 1977 another Lufthansa plane was hijacked by PFLP on behalf of the German Baader-Meinhoff terrorists and a 15-million-dollar ransom was demanded. It was not paid because West German special forces freed the passengers at Mogadishu.

The wealthiest terrorist organisation. While it is impossible to give accurate figures it is known that the PLO has an annual income of at least 800 million pounds sterling. In 1981 Saudi Arabia donated 30 million dollars.

Greatest variety of targets. Between 1968 and 1980 the PLO committed over 200 major terrorist acts in or against countries other than Israel. They attacked 40 civilian passenger aircraft, five passenger ships, 30 embassies or diplomatic missions and about the same number of economic targets, including fuel depots and factories.

It would be reasonable to assume that with such a background the nations of the world, collectively, would have set themselves against the PLO for ever. Instead, by 1980 the organisation had achieved impressive diplomatic success and acceptance. It had been allowed to open 82 offices—which in some cases have quasi-ambassadorial status—in scores of capitals and major cities. It was given a permanent office, with its own representative, at the United Nations. Its leader, Yasser Arafat, was rapturously received at the United Nations, which he addressed—and nobody seemed to object to his wearing a pistol into the chamber.

Since then Arafat has been received by many world leaders, including the Soviet president and prime minister, Chancellor Kreisky of Austria and the prime ministers of Spain, India and several other nations. He claims friendship with the former West German chancellor Willy Brandt and on one famous occasion Chancellor Schmidt telephoned Arafat to plead with him not to allow a particular incident to spoil the budding PLO–German friendship. He attends great affairs of state—such as the funeral of President Tito of Yugoslavia—where he rubs shoulders with the powerful and mighty. And in Beirut, Damascus and Baghdad he has often met Western ambassadors at official function and parties.

During 1980–81 Arafat and other PLO spokesmen were courted by either the prime ministers or foreign ministers of the European Economic Community.

The PLO became the 23rd member of the Arab League —and was recognised by it, at the Rabat Summit in 1974, as 'the sole legitimate representative of the Palestinian people.' From time to time Arafat and the PLO have incurred the hostility of King Hussein of Jordan—who waged war against the PLO in 1970—of President Gaddafi of Libya, President Sadat of Egypt, King Khaled of Saudi Arabia, President Assad of Syria and King Hassan of Morocco. The organisation and its leaders have survived all these setbacks.

Arafat helped the Ayatollah Khomeini to power in Iran, provided him with a trusted special police force and was considered one of the ayatollah's few cronies. This relationship deteriorated after the PLO supported the Soviet invasion of Afghanistan.

Beyond international politics, the PLO has won a degree of "popular" support; for instance, the PLO flag hangs in Dundee town hall and the Scottish city is twinned with Nablus, the principal city of the West Bank. The PLO has supporters, some of them devout Christians who deplore terrorism, in several Western countries.

The purpose of this book is to examine the remarkable success of the PLO in winning international recognition. There has been no phenomenon in history quite as intriguing as that of the PLO's triumph in cosmetic diplomacy.

The book does not attempt to analyse, except peripherally, the rights of the ordinary Palestinians. That they have rights and that they have suffered grievously is accepted and their plight is described in scores of books. This particular book is about those relatively few Palestinians who comprise the PLO.

Chapter Three

The Rise of the PLO

The original facts of the problem which looms like an unscaleable precipice between the PLO and Israel can be concisely expressed. In 1947 the United Nations produced a Partition Resolution which would have divided Palestine into a Jewish state and an Arab state. Jerusalem was to have special status as an internationalised city. Most Jewish leaders accepted the partition; the Arabs did not. The Arabs at this time were represented by the Arab Higher Committee, which could be said to have made an historic error of judgment in rejecting the UN recommendation for partition.

The West Bank was to go to the Palestinians but King Abdullah of Jordan seized it and in 1948 he carried out "the unification" of Arab Palestine (the West Bank) and Jordan. In several statements he made it clear that the Kingdom of Jordan was a Palestinian state.

Israel, in its declaration of independence on May 14, 1948, offered friendship—in generous language—to its Arab neighbours. It was rejected and Israel was attacked by the armies of Jordan, Egypt, Iraq and Syria, with contingents from Lebanon and Syria. As a direct consequence of the war nearly 600,000 Arabs fled from their homes while about 150,000 remained in what became the state of Israel or returned there when the fighting ended.

In the 1950s the "Palestinian issue" was in essence one of protection for a people which had never ruled itself. There was no attempt to create a mini-Palestinian state, though this would have been simple at any time between 1948 and 1967. Jordan did nothing because it was satisfied with its annexation of the West Bank; this suppressed Arab nationalism. Egypt had only an academic interest in 'Palestine,' contenting itself with military accupation of the Gaza Strip. Nevertheless in September 1948 Egypt announced the formation in Gaza of an 'All Palestinian Government,' a transparent attempt to pre-empt Jordan's claim to sovereignty. Syria claimed the whole of Palestine as 'southern Syria', a claim which the other Arab nations did not take seriously, although Syria never dropped it.

The Palestinian Arabs themselves accepted the situation of being part of Jordan. When they raided across the border of Israel they did so as Jordanians. They made no clearcut demand between 1948 and 1967 for a mini-state of their own. Other Arab powers and the Arab League had no direct interest in the Palestinian problem. Between 1948 and 1967 King Feisal of Saudi Arabia did not once worship in Jerusalem, when the Muslim holy places were in Arab hands. Not until after the 1967 war and the reunification of Jerusalem did the king say that his 'dearest wish' for 19 years had been to worship in the Holy City.

The demand for a mini-Palestinian state was not put forward seriously until after 1967 and the Israeli occupation of the West Bank and Gaza.

But by then Fatah was in action. Fatah, the first prominent guerrilla or terrorist movement, was formed from a group of Palestinians who used to meet in Gaza after 1956 and discuss how to fight Israel. Yasser Arafat became leader of this group. Organisations, like nations, reflect their leaders and the PLO is no exception. It reflects the aims and methods of Arafat, even if its constituent parts sometimes violently disagree with his dictates. Arafat himself reflects the times in which he matured. It is not possible to understand the PLO without knowing something of Arafat's background and the environment in which he developed.

Arafat was born in Gaza in 1929, his birth being registered with the Egyptian Ministry of the Interior. This has created doubt about whether he is really a Palestinian, though there are family links. Arafat's full name is Abd el-Rahman Abd el-Rauf Arafat el-Qudwa el-Husseini. Abd el-Rauf is his father's name which the Arabs customarily add to the full name and the remaining ones are his surnames. For everyday use the majority of the clan use the names el-Qudwa or Arafat el-Qudwa. Yasser Arafat has avoided mentioning his full name for it reveals his kinship to the former Grand Mufti of Jerusalem, Haj Amin el-Husseini. The Husseini family lost its status in the Arab world and if Arafat had revealed his family tree at the beginning of his career he might have endangered his underground reputation.

As a youth Arafat was involved in streetfighting and while living in Jerusalem during the years of World War II he was a member of an Arab gang which brawled with Jews in the streets and attacked Jewish shops; this brought him into conflict with the British police.

Muhammad al-Alami, son of a leading Gaza politician, remembers Arafat at school as 'a fat, moody boy who managed to frighten everyone a little. He was not like most fat boys, who tend to be buffoonish and always eager to be everyone's friend. It was always easy to be cruel to these boys. But Yasser was not like that. He played up to no one; he was shy and was always ill at ease but if you came up to him and did something or said something nasty he would just look right through you. His eyes were hypnotic and they could stop you cold.'

Hassam al-Fahum, another Gaza youth who drifted into Arafat's group, remembers that he had a great love for secrecy and mystery. 'He was all the time very serious and dedicated. He had some struggles with other boys who didn't like the idea of his leading us. There was one boy who kept belittling the el-Husseinis and Yasser himself. He tried to form a rival group, so Yasser organised five or six of us to attack the boy one day. We gave him a wicked beating and he was not heard from again. Yasser did not take part; he simply stood and watched.'

Another Gazan who knew Arafat in his youth is Taysir

al-Aref, a nephew of the great Palestinian scholar and politician, Aref el-Aref. Speaking in Cairo in 1970 Taysir el-Aref said, 'Yasser became more fanatical as he gained more confidence in himself as leader. As he became more fanatical he became more ruthless. We had perhaps forty-five members. Yasser organised us into squads of five and told us to seek out other groups and make them join us. If they refused we were to beat them into submission, and by the end of 1946 we had about three hundred boys with us.'

When Arafat's rhetoric failed he sent his 'inner circle' to deal with waverers; this group consisted of 10 boys devoted to Arafat and they would beat up those who did not show enough enthusiasm for violence.

Other firsthand evidence of Arafat, early in 1949, comes from Anway Sayigh, whose father had joined a group led by Arafat's father, Abdul. 'I didn't know Yasser very well but I used to see him roaming the streets with his brothers, all looking very severe and dedicated, searching out men who had missed meetings of the group. One day Yasser and his brothers came looking for my father who had stopped going to meetings. He was not there so they cursed me and my two brothers. We were younger than they and were properly intimidated. Then they began to bully our sisters, so we went for them. They gave us a severe beating with clubs. Yasser was particularly brutal. The others wanted to stop after they had drawn some blood but not Yasser. He continued to beat and beat us. He grew crazed by the sight of blood.'

During 1949 in Gaza much inter-tribal feuding went on, especially between the Nashashibi and el-Husseini clans, and the Nashashibis generally were the losers. Yasser Arafat and his brother Fathi were in a group with Amin Hegoub. They thought they were being trained to fight the Zionists but throughout 1949 and 1950 they did nothing but terrorise the Nashashibis and their followers. As a thinker and tactician, Arafat became leader of the squad. Hegoub recalls a mission on which about 20 young men, under Arafat, were sent to burn or cut down some orchards owned by Nashashibi interests in Gaza. There was one squad member named Hamid whom nobody really trusted. As the squad entered the orchard they were ambushed by a larger group of Nashashibi workers armed with clubs and knives and the Arafat gang was routed and all were hurt, except Hamid. Arafat accused him of betraying the gang. Hamid vehemently denied the accusation and was crying when Arafat took a pistol from behind his back and shot him in the head. 'Arafat turned to the others with a weird smile,' Hegoub says, 'and told us to take Hamid's death as a warning of what happened to a traitor.' According to Hegoub it was later found that Hamid was innocent. The raiders were betrayed by an agent of Haj Amin al-Husayni himself in the expectation that all would be killed; such a slaughter would cause a great uprising against the Nashashibi clan. Hegoub has told a Western writer that Arafat was 'not in the least bothered' by the killing of Hamid. 'I remember him saying that Hamid was the first person he had personally killed and for that reason he had served a valuable purpose.'

By 1951 Arafat had become an engineering student at Cairo University and in 1953 he joined other students in irregular operations against British troops in the Suez Canal zone. As president of the Palestine Students Federation (1952-56) he became connected with the extreme Muslim Brotherhood.

A crony of Arafat in 1953 was Walid Jiryis, who was to become well known as an oil company engineer. Arafat's election as president of the Students' Federation, Jiryis says, turned him into a 'power-maniac.' Another member of the circle around Arafat was a youth whose parents were nominally Israeli Arabs because, after 1948, they found themselves living in Israel, though at that time everybody thought the young man came from Cairo. When Arafat found out the truth he ridiculed the youth and demanded that he condemn his parents for not leaving Israel. The young man idolised Arafat but would not condemn his parents. So Arafat held a form of trial and said that as fedayeen [freedom fighters] all the group members had

27

obligations one to the other. As Jiryis recalls, Arafat made a speech along these lines, 'My heart aches for Ahmed (his real name is not now known) and my feday soul bleeds for him; we are as brothers whose blood runs from one to the other . . . But my brother Ahmed cannot bring himself to be a true feday so he must be taught.'

He therefore called forth a young man known as 'The Scimitar,' who was armed with a knife. He held down the defaulter and castrated him while Arafat sobbed bitterly. The victim killed himself that night and, according to Jiryis, it was from that moment that Arafat swore to have no friends.

He certainly had enemies at this time. During an absence in Algeria he was deposed from leadership of the Palestine Students' Federation. He retaliated by forming the General Union of Palestine Students and soon after several leaders of the PSF were found dead. In fact, Arafat was not responsible; the killings had been carried out by the Egyptian Intelligence Service, who at that time saw in Arafat a useful tool in their attempt to control the Palestinian people.

In 1956 he was a junior officer in the Egyptian army during the Suez Crisis and recent publicity claims that he saw action against British, French and Israeli troops. Whatever he might have done for Egypt during 1956 did not help him the following year when the Muslim Brotherhood, with which he was connected, was outlawed. Arafat fled from Egypt but his name remained on the government's black list until 1968.

Moving to Kuwait, Arafat became a building contractor, though he was always ready to leave his work to further his underground activities. He toured the Palestinian diaspora, preaching his gospel of 'liberation' and recruiting members for his organisation, Fatah. He likes to claim the credit for the inspiration behind the concept of Fatah but most of those who have been involved with it from its beginnings claim that credit belongs primarily to the intellectual Khalid al-Hassan and secondly to Khalid al-Wazir.

Arafat considered himself a representative of the 'Generation of Revenge,' taking over leadership from those who had led the 'Generation of Disaster.' The contrast with disaster and the very idea of revenge attracted a good many young idealists to Arafat. He became their leader by a curious process of selection, which his friend Salah Khalaf describes: 'There is a special reason for choosing Abu Ammar . . . that is, of us all he is the least garrulous. Actually the idea was to announce three names as official spokesmen but they all refused. Since Abu Ammar [Arafat's code-name] was the only absent one, he was chosen. The decision was publicly announced and he could not but accept.'

Arafat and his aides set up cells in Kuwait and among Arab students in West Germany and they started a training camp in Algeria.

Tempestuous and vehement, inflexible, and at times illmannered, Arafat was a violent leader. In one incident a new recruit rushed forwards and kissed his hand. Arafat punched him on the head, kicked him and shouted, 'What are you smacking your lips for? We're all equal!'

Travelling in Europe, the Middle East and China, Arafat worked at creating political links with student groups and left-wing cells. In 1965 he began to win control of the refugee camps in Lebanon and Jordan and in the PLO itself. There is much evidence to show that he gained control by coercion and terrorism.

As Arafat stood before the UN General Assembly in November 1974 and accepted its clamorous ovation he was to many of the delegates an appealing figure, even a romantic one. The khaki windbreaker, carefully kept soiled, the checked head-dress, the holster on his hip—he was the Third World underdog fighting back. His speech was the product of the minds of several close Fatah colleagues and it was a masterpiece, a confection, as Thomas Kiernan says,* 'of truths and untruths, historical

* In his biography of Arafat, 1976, Kiernan's researches into Arafat's background were extensive and his account is authoritative. My own researches substantiate Kiernan's. Arafat has never denied or sought to 'correct' any statement made about him.

accuracies and inaccuracies, threats and mollifications' —delivered in contrasting pleading and then passionate Arabic. And at the end came the image of the gun and the olive branch. If Arafat had not been a world figure before that speech in November 1974 he certainly was afterwards —though the world knew very little about the man himself and the organisation he represented.

One of the greatest PLO propaganda coups has been the selling of Yasser Arafat as a 'moderate'. The propaganda success is evident in that the Western media had come, by 1975, to use the adjective 'moderate' whenever it used Arafat's name. Similarly, Western politicians made the same habitual coupling. Because Arafat is a world figure his claim should be subjected to examination.

Some of his own statements hardly indicate moderation. In 1971 he was saying flatly, 'No, we do not want peace. We want war and victory. Peace for us means the destruction of Israel and nothing else.' (*Esquire*, Buenos Aires, March 21, 1971)

'The Palestine resistance constitutes a single body which is fighting for a single purpose,' Arafat told the Middle East newsagency on September 7, 1972. His point here is that the 'single purpose'—the destruction of Israel—is worth any amount of bloodshed.

To the *Philadelphia Inquirer* (November 28, 1975) he said: 'We do not want to destroy any people. It is precisely because we have been advocating co-existence that we have shed so much blood.' His point seems to be that the goal of co-existence justifies great bloodshed.

In an NBC interview, February 8, 1976, Arafat said, 'We are not against civilians; we are doing our best to avoid civilians.' This repetition of the message of moderation has had a greater impact than the PLO's attacks, which in fact have been almost entirely against civilian targets.

Usually dressed in soiled khaki and wearing a checked khaffiyah he increasingly became the prize of Arab journalists who sought him out for interviews in underground locations. They presented him as he wanted to be presented, living an austere life of physical hardship and personal sacrifice. 'I am married to Fatah,' he was often quoted as saying. 'Fatah is my woman, my family, my life.'

When he saw the effect the newspaper stories were having he wrapped around himself other cloaks of mystery and danger. He refused to talk about his early life, saying 'I was not born until I became Abu Ammar.' He even threatened death to any Arab journalist who mentioned his blood relationship to Haj Amin, the Grand Mufti. 'I am the Palestine people,' he said. 'And the Palestinian people are me. It makes no difference who I am, it is what I am that matters. Any Palestinian could be Abu Ammar, therefore Abu Ammar is all Palestinians.'

Coming into contact with more and more reporters Arafat came to appreciate the value of being enigmatic. In particular the Arab journalists delighted in irony, contradiction, unpredictability, and in bold, forthright declarations.

To the *Kuwaiti Weekly* (April 11, 1977) he said: 'I am not a man of settlements and concessions. I will struggle till the last inch of Palestine is returned . . . our struggle in the occupied land will be violently and bitterly escalated. We will start with the stepping up of our suicide strikes against the Zionist enemy . . . I will let the fedayeen's actions speak for themselves.'

In April 1979 he was asked whether President Carter, President Sadat and Prime Minister Begin would get any assistance from the Palestinians in negotiations on the West Bank. He replied: 'They can ask the masses. Demonstrations, resistance, uprisings is our reply. Our people is our time bomb against this conspiracy. My people will deal with anyone who joins the negotiations.'

In an interview in August 1979 Arafat was asked if he would say that the PLO leadership was more or less in the hands of moderates. 'We are freedom fighters,' he replied, and would not enlarge on this statement. Asked if he could be a freedom fighter and a moderate at the same time, Arafat said, 'If you consider my struggle for my people a

31

moderate attitude then I am a moderate. I am controlled by one line and that is the interest of my people, without concessions to Israel.'

While Arafat's grasp of international politics was for a long time simplistic and ingenuous he had a sure touch within the PLO. Abu Daoud, a planner of the 1972 Munich Olympics massacre of Israeli athletes, complained in 1980 that 'Arafat manages to exploit the differences between progressives and conservatives to outshout or outshoot his rivals.'

Arafat's moods vary greatly but he often appears buoyantly confident and enthusiastically aggressive. He answers an interviewer's questions with another question, generally rhetorical but sometimes as an evasive measure. To a question on how negotiations for peace should start, Arafat said, 'Negotiations with whom? Definitely we are searching for peace and we consider that peace can best be settled through the United Nations.' His 20,000 Fatah fighters cannot hope to defeat Israel's military might but, as Arafat once told me, they have 'veto power' over any propositions made for peace in the Middle East.

Arafat is humourless but when with journalists he is often expansive and warm and makes a great fuss of any other PLO men who happen to be present. Several PLO men have told me privately that Arafat treats them in such a way only when journalists are there; otherwise he is at best distant and often cold.

He has always understood the need for a rousing slogan. One of his most effective slogans—'There is nothing greater than to die for Palestine's return'—is aimed at the teenage boys of the training camps. Arafat is not a 'good' Muslim by the standards of the mullahs and ayatollahs but he uses the injunctions or exhortations of the Koran when they suit his purpose—and never more than when encouraging martyrdom. Martyrdom, says the Koran, is the surest way to paradise, and Arafat repeats the teaching tirelessly. The way to paradise lies through East Jerusalem and if a young man dies striving for the return of the eastern part of the city to Arab hands he will be a martyr among martyrs. When Arafat visits the refugee camps, often to deliver an impassioned speech to a new intake of guerrillas, a guard of honour greets him as a head of state. In Shatila refugee camp I saw a bagpipe band play him onto the parade ground, where he delivered yet another 'martyrdom for Palestine' speech, which the young men received with great acclaim.

Another foundation member of Fatah was Salah Khalaf (underground name Abu Iyad). A teacher and playwright, Khalaf said that Fatah represented a group of Palestinian youth 'disgusted by the disunity of the Arab world.'

It is Khalaf, in the 1980s, who guards Fatah's flank from hostile Arabs and Israeli assassination squads. Chief of a tough security unit and idol of many Fatah militants, Khalaf worries in private about his own strongman reputation. He has two apprehensions—that he is not as 'strong' as his reputation purports and that he does not really want to be a 'strongman' but a diplomat. A third early member of Fatah is Khalil al-Wazir (underground name Abu Jihad), who was to become Fatah's military chief. An efficient organiser, he retains a tight hand on Fatah's extensive military apparatus but also masterminds many of the PLO overtures to United States public opinion. Another key personality with long service is Farouk Khaddoumi (Abu Lutf) who renounced a background more well to do than others to become a Fatah organiser. A bland and often persuasive diplomat, he acts as PLO 'foreign minister' and trains new ranks of Fatah recruits in public relations.

The title 'Fatah' is the reversed initials, in Arabic, for Movement for the Liberation of Palestine Harakat al-Tahrir al-Watani al-Filistini (watani = national). As it happens, fatah itself is an Arabic word meaning conquest.

From 1959 the organisation's ideas were given publicity in a 30-page monthly journal edited in Kuwait and entitled *Falastinuna (Our Palestine)*. Cells were set up in Kuwait, among Palestinian students in West Germany, and training began in Algeria. In that year too President Nasser and General Qassem of Iraq were using the term "Palestinian entity"; both wanted to arouse the million Palestinians in Jordan to undermine the Hashemite crown.

In September 1963 the Arab League Council invited Ahmed Shukeiri to Cairo to lead a revival of the "Palestinian entity." Shukeiri, a fiery demagogue and at one time Saudi Arabian delegate to the UN, worked out plans for founding the Palestine Liberation Organisation and the Palestine Liberation Army. On May 22, 1964 he opened, in East Jerusalem, the first Palestine National Congress.

But he achieved little unity. Six large anti-Israel groups set up a rival union, Fatah retained its independence and most of the small groups resisted assimilation.

But the Arab government leaders supported Shukeiri, especially Nasser who apparently saw in the PLO the solution to restoring his declining influence among the Palestinians. Fatah, through *Our Palestine*, wanted action and not rhetoric and urged Nasser to go to war against Israel. If the Arab states would do nothing else then they could 'surround Palestine with a preventive belt of defences and watch the battle between Fatah and the Israelis.'

Shukeiri announced that only the Palestine Liberation Army, a regular army formation, could authorise any military action and denounced Fatah. At this time Arafat was in prison, put there by Lebanese security officers for organising a raid into Israel to damage a water pipeline. He came out to find that the raid had been abortive but that it had excited praise from Arab press and radio.

Arafat set up headquarters in Damascus. In June 1965 Fatah delegates to the Palestine National Congress in Cairo met the world's press for the first time and expressed their policy with startling directness—'To entangle the Arab nations in a war with Israel.'

The Arab governments were alarmed by Fatah's raids. In May 1966 the Syrian Government, under General Jedid, tried to take control of Fatah and assigned Captain Yussuf Urabi, an officer in the regular Palestinian units of the Syrian Army, to take control of Fatah from inside. Arafat's assassins killed Urabi in Yarmuk refugee camp.

Amid plots and counter-plots a stronger group emerged —the Heroes of the Return, founded by the Arab Nationalists. The Jordanians sent assassins to kill Shafik el-Hut, a member of the Heroes and head of the PLO's branch in Beirut.

With typical rhetoric Shukeiri announced: 'The PLO no longer consists of dreams and hopes. The PLO is now a fighting revolutionary organisation, professing action and self-sacrifice, followed by the brave fedayeen warriors. . . . The fedayeen will strike Israel . . . they will leap forth from every hill and every wadi, from Aqaba in the south to Golan in the north. From now on our operations will not cease. Our heroes are prepared to open two fronts, one in Amman, the other in Tel Aviv. . . . Both our fields and theirs will be set on fire. There will be more than one battle. There will be a day for the Knesset, for the Hebrew University, for Natanya, for Tel Aviv, and occupied Jerusalem. Blood and bullets will be the only exchange between us and the enemy.'

Despite Shukeiri's bombast the PLO and Fatah played no particular part in the Six-Day War of June 1967 except that Fatah men gave covering fire to the retreating Syrian forces on the Golan Heights. But with the Arab armies discredited and Nasser's prestige low, Fatah moved quickly to fill the vacuum by gaining control over the million Palestinians now under Israeli rule. Also, Fatah squads hurried to collect battlefield booty before the Israeli salvage squads got to it.

Perhaps the most important development that year was the formation, in November, of the Popular Front for the Liberation of Palestine, under Dr. George Habash. PFLP developed from an Egyptian-sponsored programme to promote subversion against other Arab governments and thus increase Egypt's authority. In December 1967 a Syrian puppet, the Palestine Liberation Front, under Ahmed Jibril, linked with PFLP. And in April 1968 an official Syrian terrorist group, Sa'ika (Thunderbolt), made its debut.

With more manpower and better training Fatah became

the dominant guerrilla group; in all during 1968 there were 992 anti-Israeli incidents—though many were negligible—and Fatah was responsible for the majority.

While other Arab bodies were painfully re-assessing themselves, Habash and his colleagues abandoned the Arab bourgeoisie and turned their activities to the working class. They proclaimed themselves to be a Marxist-Leninist movement; Habash saw the terrorist movement not only as the forerunner of a struggle against Israel but the nucleus of a profound social revolution in the entire Arab world. He brought the Popular Front into being to operate as the extreme left of the terrorist movement. With this and two other groups he had created, Heroes of the Return and the Youth of Revenge, he tried to counter-act Fatah's growing power. Habash and his assistants launched a powerful propaganda campaign against it. The choice of priorities—anti-Fatah rather than anti-Israeli —might seem irrational; it can be explained on the grounds that Israel is a means to an end not an end in itself.

In-fighting now reached extreme proportions. Habash was imprisoned in Damascus and the PFLP was fragmented again. Habash escaped in November 1968 and returned to his headquarters in Amman to find a rebellion on his hands. Two of his chief assistants, Nayef Hawatmeh and Salah Rafat, had accused the absent Habash of being 'a Fascist demagogue.' In retaliation Habash men in the refugee camps beat up Hawatmeh men. Hawatmeh accused the Habash gang of torturing and killing members of his own group. Hawatmeh, now leading the Iraq-backed Popular Democratic Front for the Liberation of Palestine (PDFLP), called a great conference of leaders of all kinds of Palestinian organisations to condemn the "Fascist methods, stained in blood" of the Popular Front. The PDFLP absorbed the Palestine Revolutionary Left League and the Popular Organisation for the Liberation of Palestine.

Had it been left to Fatah to wage a fedayeen war it is just possible that over a long period it might have achieved

36

some of its aims and the world image of Palestinian "resistance" may have been better. Most prominent of the extreme groups was the PFLP. Against the background of intrigue and violence it is easier to understand the operations of PFLP, whose actions have often seemed more designed to embarrass Arab governments than the Israeli enemy. For instance, PFLP saboteurs blew up the oil pipeline carrying Saudi Arabian oil to the Mediterranean; the Saudis attacked PFLP as "operating in the service of the devil."

Habash's theory was always that to kill a Jew far from the battlefield had more effect than killing a hundred Jews in battle. "When we set fire to a store in London (referring to the incendiary bombs in Marks and Spencer, August 17, 1969) those few flames are worth the burning down of two kibbutzim." he said.

By May 1970 PFLP had come into the PLO fold, if only because the PLO had financial power—the money which came from powerful backers, such as Saudi Arabia and Libya, to be disbursed to the various groups.

Despite this apparent stabilisation, proliferation of factions within the PLO continued and in 1974 the executive committee was enlarged from 9 to 14. Even then, not all the smaller groups are represented on the executive.

Organisation	Leader	Representatives
Fatah	Arafat (also head of PLO)	2
PFLP	Habash	1
PDFLP	Hawatmeh	1
Popular Front General Command	Jibril	1
Sa'ika	Zohair Mohsen, until his assassination	1
Palestine (or Arab Liberation Army)	Formerly part of the Egyptian regular army now sponsored by Syria and led by a Syrian	

Ostensibly the PLO is a distinctly Palestinian-Arab institution but it is really merged inseparably with various other Arab groups. At Arab League meetings it participates as if representing a 23rd Arab state, but in its own councils, it must seek consensus among the Palestinian factions and bodies which represent the official policy of various Arab states—Syria, Iraq, Libya, Kuwait, Yemen, Saudi Arabia. This policy is in turn influenced by that of the Soviet Union, especially in Syria's case.

The PLO was not created by demand of the Palestinian Arabs; they have never participated in choosing the leaders of the PLO or in formulation of policy. There is a PLO legislature or council of 100 members which includes members from many walks of life, but it meets only twice a year and its members dare not form groups or factions which might be seen as hostile to the cabinet or executive. The importance of the council is its existence—it helps the Arab world to recognise the PLO as the only legitimate representative of the Arab Palestinians. And it is this recognition which, in turn, gives the PLO its impressive status.

Chapter Four

Unswerving Aims

As the PLO has consisted at times of up to 40 organisations it occasionally accommodates men who deviate from the official line. But the central point is that the declared direction of the organisation and the overriding objective of its leadership remain unchanged: the elimination of the State of Israel. Each time the PLO issues a statement whose extremist content is uncertain an expectation of possible peace permeates the Free World, as though the terrorists had moderated their stand. Thus, when the PLO council met in Cairo in March, 1977, some observers believed that the session would amend those provisions of the organisation's Covenant which entail the dismembering of Israel. Instead, the PLO reaffirmed its goal. Hani el Hasan, a member of the central committee, made a special statement to explain the situation. Interviewed by United Press International in the Egyptian capital on March 16, he said: 'Who would dare ask for an amendment of the PLO Charter? Arafat himself would kill him.'

Despite this and similar 'clarifications,' the international community has been unable to draw the obvious conclusions from PLO extremism and persists in maintaining that the organisation is about to adopt a different position. On May 12, 1977, for example, only two months after the PLO council decision in Cairo, the *New York Times* reported evidence of a 'new PLO attitude toward Israel.' Over successive months, this opinion grew in scope, and it was coupled with demands that Israel become 'flexible' and 'compromising'. Then, in early September, 1977, the PLO convened a conference in Damascus and rejected Security Council Resolution 242 as a basis for political negotiations in the Middle East conflict. This uncompromising stance was contrary to statements by Western statesmen, Arab leaders—and even PLO spokesmen themselves—implying that the organisation was about to adopt a less extreme position, including tacit recognition of Israel's right to exist.

The statements and resolutions emanating from the Damascus meeting indicate that, far from altering its position, the PLO reiterated the primary objective stated in its Covenant—the destruction of the State of Israel. Once again, the gap was revealed between vague pronouncements issued to ensure media attention, and real intentions.

PLO strategic policy and its fundamental aims are contained in the Palestine National Covenant, first drawn up in 1964 and revised in July 1969 after the Fatah take-over of the PLO. Since it is the quasi constitution of the PLO and because it is recognised by Arab governments and many other states as embodying the legitimate demands of the PLO it must be taken seriously. It contains 33 articles and they fall into three main groups. They are:

a. *Positive Palestinian Claims*
   Articles *1–18* assert the Arab claim to Palestine, define who is a "Palestinian", assert the Palestinian obligation to liberate Palestine, and Palestinian interdependency with the Arab World. They conclude with an appeal to all mankind to help the Palestinians in their struggle to liberate Palestine.
b. *Negative Claims*
   Articles *19–23* contain a denial of Jewish and of international rights, reject any compromise over Palestine, and elaborate the intrinsic evil of Israel and its Jewish citizens.
c. *Constitution of the PLO*

Articles 24–33 describe the function of the PLO for the achievement of the Covenant's aims, and assert that the liberation of Palestine cannot be subordinated to any other aim.

These are the key articles:

Article 1 "Palestine is the homeland of the Palestinian Arab people and an integral part of the great Arab homeland, and the people of Palestine is a part of the Arab Nation." Palestine is defined as the territory included in the Mandate.

Article 3 "The Palestinian Arab people possesses the legal right to its homeland, and when the liberation of its homeland is completed it will exercise self-determination solely according to its own will and choice".

This article is contrary to the PLO slogan which calls for the establishment in Palestine of a "secular democratic state".

The Arab Palestinians cannot logically both assert their exclusive domination in Palestine *and* claim that their state will be democratic.

Article 9 "Armed struggle is the only way to liberate Palestine and is therefore a strategy and not tactics."

This article shows that diplomatic initiatives, compromise and dialogue are dismissed as alternatives to violence.

Article 15 "The liberation of Palestine, from an Arab viewpoint, is a national duty to repulse the Zionist, imperialist invasion from the great Arab homeland and to purge the Zionist presence from Palestine." The PLO state cannot be democratic if one section of its population is to be "purged".

Article 16 "Jews who were living permanently in Palestine until the beginning of the Zionist invasion will be considered Palestinians".

For Israelis this is a most ominous clause because it means that nearly three million Jews in Israel will not be considered Palestinians and will therefore have no rights to remain. Those who do remain will not have the same rights as Palestinians, being only 'considered' as such.

Article 19 "The partitioning of Palestine in 1947 and the establishment of Israel is fundamentally null and void, whatever time has elapsed. . . .'

Article 20 "The Balfour Declaration, the Mandate Document, and what has been based upon them are considered null and void. The claim of a historical or spiritual tie between Jews and Palestine does not tally with historical realities nor with the constituents of statehood in their true sense. Judaism, in its character as a religion of revelation, is not a nationality with an independent existence. Likewise, the Jews are not one people with an independent personality. They are rather citizens of the states to which they belong'.

These two articles reveal a rejection of historical and contemporary realities. This rejection is fundamental to the Covenant otherwise the PLO would logically be obliged to concede that the Jews too have rights in the Land and that a compromise would be the just solution.

Article 22 "Zionism is a political movement organically related to world imperialism and hostile to all movements of liberation and progress in the world. It is a racist and fanatical movement in its formation; aggressive, expansionist and colonialist in its aims. . . ."

This clause is a logical outcome of the denial of Jewish national identity. It echoes the Czarist anti-Semitic myth that Jews conspired to dominate the world. Hence the statement that Zionism is an "imperialist" movement. This clause is designed to attract the support and sympathy of Third World states and their Soviet ally. There is no credible evidence for the claims in this article, which has echoes of Nazi anti-semitic propaganda.

There is nothing in the 33 Articles of the Covenant as interpreted by the Palestine National Council in March 1977 which suggests that the PLO and its supporters do not intend the fulfilment of their aims.

Farouk Khaddoumi has many times repeated the PLO's policy in unambiguous and succinct terms. "No Palestinian leader would think of recognising Israel or of amending the Palestinian Charter." (*) And: "The

(*) UPI, Cairo, March 16, 1977

Palestine Liberation Organisation will never recognise Israel—even if Israel recognises the PLO." (*) And again: "The PLO will not recognise Israel, even if an independent Palestinian state is established." (**)

The Fatah Congress held in Damascus in June 1980 confirmed the very hard line. The 500 delegates ratified a political programme defining Fatah's aim as being "to liberate Palestine completely, and to liquidate the Zionist entity politically, economically, militarily, culturally and ideologically.' This Fatah language is far harsher than that of the PLO and omits the previous PLO provision that only those Jews resident in Palestine before the 1948 creation of Israel should be allowed to remain in the new state. The result of the congress—only the fourth in Fatah's history—was to back Arafat's hard line for the PLO.

The Fatah Congress of 1980 did not *create* this line: Arafat had never deviated from it. In Beirut on March 12, 1979 he told Associated Press, "The people will continue to fuel the torch of the revolution with rivers of blood until the whole of the occupied homeland is liberated . . . not just part of it."

In February 1980 Arafat, in Venezuela, had given the PLO's aims in detail, perhaps not expecting his words to be translated in Europe:

'Peace for us means the destruction of Israel. We are preparing for an all-out war, a war which will last for generations . . . We shall not rest until the day when we return to our home, and until we destroy Israel . . . The destruction of Israel is the goal of our struggle, and the guidelines of that struggle have remained firm since the establishment of Fatah in 1965.

(*) *Deutsches Fernsehen*, West Germany, August 12, 1979
(**) *Al Watan*, Kuwait, October 18, 1979

1. Revolutionary violence is the only means for the liberation of the land of our fathers.

2. The goal of that violence is the destruction of Zionism in all its political, economic and military forms and its expulsion from Palestine.

3. Our revolutionary activity must remain independent of any party or state control.

4. This action will be one of long duration. We know that the intention of some of the Arab leaders is to solve the conflict by peaceful means. When this occurs we shall oppose it.'*

The fifteenth Palestine National Council congress held in Damascus in April 1981 was anticipated by the West in the hope that some tone of realistic compromise might be established and by the Arab states for a different reason: They wanted to see who would hold the balance of power in the 15-man central committee.

Arafat himself had to prove to the congress that he had been able to extract political concessions from the West without conceding anything to Israel. That he achieved this was shown by the willingness of Habash and the PFLP to rejoin the central committee. Habash had resigned in 1974 to start the 'Rejectionist Front'; what it rejected was Arafat's "Diplomatic alternative." At that time Arafat argued that diplomacy should for the time being have greater weight than massed or armed struggle; he was proved right in that Europe by 1981 had moved a long way towards recognising the PLO. The National Council criticised the "European initiative" but it nevertheless confirmed Arafat's plans to continue his contacts with European leaders.

Habash agreed, after much persuasion by Arafat and others, that he would accept "a Palestine" on the West Bank and Gaza strip. He insisted on adding, to Arafat's irritation, that he would accept this "as a first step." Privately this is Arafat's position but he knows that

* *El Mundo*, Caracas, 11 February 1980.

tactically to make such a qualification publicly is damaging.

Even though the PFLP was re-admitted two of the smaller and even more extreme organisations were not —the Palestinian Liberation Front under "Abu Abbas" and backed by Libya and Iraq and the pro-Iraq Popular Struggle Front headed by Dr. Samir Ghoushi. They were seen as internally divisive. Fatah was able to increase its representation to three—Arafat, Farouk Khaddoumi and Mahmoud Abbas; with the six independent members who consistently support Fatah, Arafat thus controls the 15-man "Cabinet" or Executive Committee.

One of the most interesting resolutions of the 1981 congress was the call for "general Palestinian mobilisation." The call is not new and is fraught with practical difficulties since it is dependent on the goodwill of many host countries. The demand for military mobilisation was made in almost the same breath as strident criticism of King Hussein for refusing to allow military operations against Israel from his territory. For Arafat, though, there was a more practical consideration: like Che Guevara, Arafat knows that guerilla-type forces cannot survive if kept idle. In one way or another they must be given "movement," as in southern Lebanon, and they must grow. Following the mobilisation call came another resolution to set up a joint command to co-ordinate training, supplies and ancillary services.

'Mobilisation' also reflected the anticipation among Palestinians and within the PLO that some solution to their problem was in the offing and that the time had therefore come to set about building the organs of the Palestinian state. High on the list is a regular army to confront Israel.

In one speech Arafat cried that "Our revolution was born not merely to survive but to become victorious." This had a plaintive tone after 17 years of intense terrorist activity with little to show but a greater number of Palestinian casualties than Israeli casualties. The 1973 war proved that the struggle in the Middle East is between conventional armies; terrorism and incursions have no military impact—though they do much to ensure that no political dialogue can take place.

The Palestine National Council is said to be an example of 'democracy in action'; this it is in that its membership represents all sections of the Palestinian community. But all members must be acceptable to the PLO, so that the democratic process is pre-selective and not what would be demanded in the West. The congress increased the numbers of representatives from the West Bank and Gaza from 102 to 184. This was largely a tactical change as few of these delegates could be expected to attend congress and if they do their status would be that of observers without voting rights. A number of West Bank Palestinians have complained—though necessarily in private—that the West Bank and Gaza should have more say in the process of Palestinian decision-making. The PLO leaders are wary of granting local Palestinians more power for fear of what they refer to as *qiyada badilla*—substitute leadership by moderate Palestinians.

The National Council is supposed to be "independent" but its credibility was damaged by a major blunder in the London-produced *Free Palestine* in May 1981,* in an article about the functioning of the Council. "The PNC is the most important of the institutions within the PLO, and is widely seen as being the Palestinian parliament. Constitutionally, the Council is the supreme authority, formulating policies and programmes for the PLO. . . ." The use of the word *within*, though accurate, was evidently a mistake; the usual line is to present the PLO as subservient to the Council. For instance, the Council is said to elect the Palestinian "Cabinet" or Executive Committee. In fact, the PLO controls the Council—as *within* indicates—which then for cosmetic reasons "elects" the "Cabinet" proposed by the PLO. It was no surprise then that Arafat was re-elected Chairman of the Cabinet, and that others re-elected were Farouk Khaddoumi, Abdul-

* Page 5, Column 3.

Rahim Ahmad (Arab Liberation Front), Yasir Abd Rab-buh (DFLP), Talal Naji (PFLP—General Command) and Abd al-Muhsin Abu Mayser (PNF).

It was clear to the Arab veteran observers who studied the eight days of debates and speeches at the Palestinian National Council's 15th congress that the PLO would become more radical. One factor was the return of Habash and the PFLP; Habash, though ailing, was still fiery, and his group had a seat, held by the militant Ahmad al-Yamani, in the Cabinet. The first of the PFLP's "Six Principles" of 1968 is that 'The only language that the enemy will understand is revolutionary violence.' And the fourth principle: 'Armed resistance is the only effective method available to the masses.'

The second factor bringing about a more radical PLO stance was perhaps the more significant. It was made clear to the PNC congress that the PLO had achieved near-recognition by Europe without any need for a demonstration of real moderation. Thus, many speakers argued, the PLO could be "less moderate" without offending the Europeans.

The congress, widely reported in Israel, left Israelis even less able than before to believe in the PLO's integrity and in what it has referred to at times as a 'secular, multi-national, democratic state.' How could any of these conditions be achieved, Israelis ask, if their blood is to 'run in rivers'?

We are left, then, with the interesting question of how the PLO, despite its countless aggressive statements and equally numerous attacks with bombs and rockets, has managed to convince the world at large that it is a moderate organisation with peaceful political aims.

Chapter Five

The Multi-Barrel Propaganda Weapon

On March 17, 1980 the British Foreign Secretary, Lord Carrington, made the statement that he did not believe 'that the PLO, as such, is a terrorist organisation,' though he conceded that there were "some elements of the PLO which in the past have been associated with the terrorists."*

Two days later I had occasion to visit the Jordanian Embassy in London where a military attaché brought Lord Carrington's speech into our conversation. 'If the PLO needs proof that propaganda is worth all the money they spend on it, here it is,' he said. 'It's easy to get the Third World to believe anything you tell them and not all that difficult to work many Americans around [to the PLO's point of view] but the British Foreign Office is usually more cautious and to get it to make a statement like this is priceless. It will influence the whole of Western Europe.'

The attaché probably knew that the PLO did not need proof of the effectiveness of its propaganda; its efficacy had been shown many times and in many ways before March 1980. Earlier that very month President Giscard d' Estaing of France, while on a Middle East tour, had called for

* Three days later, the Minister of State at the Foreign Office, Douglas Hurd, made a part-disclaimer of his chief's statement. The PLO was an umbrella organisation which did contain terrorist elements. This important qualification did not receive much publicity.

'Palestinian self-determination'—a phrase often used in PLO propaganda.

PLO propaganda has the simple and direct aim to sell the PLO as a moderate, non-violent, reasonable and democratically representative body while convincing the world that the Israelis are "intransigent", cruel, bigoted, destructive, racist.

The methods by which these aims are achieved were set out for me in 1972 by Ibrahim al-Abid when he was director of the PLO Research Centre, Beirut. The basic factors are 'slogans, photographs, insinuations, spectacle, documents, tears and smiles,' he said. Clearly he had learned from the methods used by Goebbels, Mao Tse-Tung and American presidential candidates. Al-Abid referred to the Eisenhower campaigning slogan, 'I like Ike,' which he regarded as 'simplicity at its best.' And he quoted 'Ein folk, ein faterland, ein führer' as another effective slogan. Al-Abid's principles of propaganda were sound but in practice in 1972 PLO propaganda was relatively crude and could be measured in weight—a massive output of pamphlets, magazines and books, many of them written in a dull, heavy way unsuitable for use in the West.

Then PLO sympathisers in the West explained to its leaders that they could put their case most effectively by winning the support of Western students, academics, churchmen, politicians and journalists—in that order of priority—the students being the most impressionable and the journalists the least. Also, these Western experts advised, the PLO must moderate its public pronouncements, no matter what was said in private discussion. For instance, in 1970, Fatah announced:

> The aim of this war is not to impose our will on the enemy but to destroy him in order to take his place (ifna'uhu lil-hululi mahallahu). In a conventional war there is no need to continue the war if the enemy submits to our will . . . while in a people's war there is no deterrent, for its aim is not to subjugate the

enemy but to destroy (ifna') him. A conventional war has limited aims which cannot be transcended, for it is necessary to allow the enemy to exist in order to impose our will over him, while in a people's war destruction of the enemy is the first and last duty.*

A British member of parliament cautioned Arafat against permitting such extravagant language. Fatah could safely talk about 'bad Zionists" but should concede that there were "good Jews". Similarly, destruction of the Jewish enemy would not find sympathy in Europe; it would be better if Fatah could announce its acceptance in Palestine of "ordinary Jews" while those who were unable to live in peace with the Palestinians could leave without threat or hindrance.

As the PLO became wealthy it was able to hire the services of skilled Western propagandists, all of whom pointed out that some of the best propaganda would come from foreigners who could be convinced of the justness of the Palestinians' cause. Clerics and academics were the best material to work on because they had the 'credibility of sincerity' in their own countries.

While some influential PLO men accepted this advice others were still thinking in terms of violence directed not only against Israelis in Israel but against Israeli targets elsewhere in the world, and against Western targets, such as airlines. This was the hijack era, the period of indiscriminate terror aimed at producing worldwide publicity for the PLO. This attitude gave way gradually—though never completely—to propaganda and "peace offensives" and to a sweep of diplomatic activity, itself a form of propaganda, never seen before from any non-government organisation. PLO men have told me that it was "surprisingly easy" to recruit priests and students to their cause, though 'recruit' is perhaps misleading since many of them are unworldly and not conscious of having been recruited.

* Voice of Fatah, February 18, 1970, quoted from BBC Monitoring Service

One man of this type is Father Lucas Grollenberg, a Dutch Dominican who wrote a book called *Palestine Comes First*.

Grollenberg and his publishers honestly state their intentions on the cover of the book. 'It is a story which makes chilling reading. . . . How modern Israel has been built up on exploitation and deceit. . . .' There is no temporising here, no balancing of arguments and no analysis of historic cause and effect. Even the translator is allowed to write an almost polemical preface, with a reference to the "so-called Camp David Peace Agreement." To dismiss the greatest Middle East peace achievement since 1948 with a derisory "so-called" shows a strange ignorance.

Father Grollenberg is a sincere writer, commendably concerned about the Palestinians, and his integrity is not in question. But, as with other sincere and ingenuous men, some of his sources are questionable, especially the PLO propaganda office in Beirut. He says, for instance, that 'Israeli children are taught that there never was a Palestine . . . It has always been Eretz Israel, the land of Israel.' This is not only inflammatory but untrue; the reality of Palestine is a fundamental of Israeli schooling, which Father Grollenberg could have found out from a glance at any primary school history textbook.

He quotes from George Antonius' great book *The Arab Awakening*: "The places which are most sacred to Christians—those having to do with Jesus—and which are also sacred to the Moslems—are not only not sacred to the Jews but abhorrent to them." This is not true; tens of thousands of Christian clerics who have visited Israel have commented on the reverence of the Israelis towards the holy shrines and places of all the religions. In any case, Antonius' book was written in 1938 before there ever was a state of Israel, so to use an extract from it in 1980 without some qualification is misleading.

Writing about the 1948 Arab-Israeli War, Grollenberg says that defeat for the Arabs was inevitable, partly because the Israeli soldiers were better trained. This is the

PLO's propaganda line. In fact, there were *no* Israeli soldiers in the accepted military sense. Most were refugees from Europe, they were ragged and ill-equipped and many had no military training. No military historian concedes that the Arabs' defeat was inevitable on the grounds of Israeli military superiority.

In places Grollenberg presents PLO distortion–propaganda. 'At the beginning of 1976 tensions in Lebanon which had been increasing over the years led to a violent civil war, yet one more consequence of the Zionist state.' He means 'as a consequence of the Palestinians being displaced nearly 30 years before,' but the average reader of the book could infer that the "Zionists" engineered the Lebanon Civil War, which they did not.

Fed on PLO propaganda by persuasive people the priest's crusading compassion obscures his judgment. In effect he admits as much in the most significant of all his statements. '. . . I had hesitations about an English translation; the book had been written in 1970, in far too much of a hurry, and more on the basis of incidental reading than systematic research; its subject matter was outside the sphere of my specialist competence, because I am neither an historian nor a political scientist.'

All four propositions in this sentence are obvious. Despite the shortcomings to which Father Grollenberg confesses, he *did* publish, thus helping to misrepresent the Palestinian issue. To be so intellectually irresponsible as to write about such a serious and far-reaching theme on the basis of 'incidental reading' is a measure of the effectiveness of PLO propaganda.

Students, even more easily moulded by the PLO's propagandists, have provided much publicity—but only at student level. Taken on arranged tours, students of scores of nationalities have returned to their own lands to write passionately about the Palestinians—and equally vehemently about Israel, though without visiting that country. PLO men concede that students overreact in what they write for university journals and papers but as they expect a long-term yield this is not worrying. 'Today's student could be working in a foreign ministry in five years,' a PLO man in Paris told me. And as such he would be an investment.

But it is at political level that the PLO spends most energy and money. To create an organisation which can influence a political party or a government is a worthwhile achievement, while to penetrate a ministry or reach a minister himself is a triumph.

The PLO's propaganda success in Western Europe at government level is the result of an approach supposedly evolved by Arafat himself; it was more probably suggested to him by a particular British member of parliament. Homegrown or imported, the aim was simple—to ease the embarrassment which democratic governments might feel in speaking to the PLO. The international two-track solution was equally simple—the PLO must assume an image of reputable diplomacy while deputing terrorist activities to its member organisations.

Arafat's first propaganda breakthrough in what the French call his 'charm offensive' was in Vienna in July 1979 when he was received by the Austrian Chancellor, Bruno Kreisky, in the company of the former German Chancellor, Willy Brandt. Since they welcomed him in their role as leaders of the Socialist International as well as in their national role, this was a double triumph. But such acceptance had not happened overnight. Having learned from its agents in Austria that Kreisky, though a Jew, was anti-Zionist, PLO Intelligence subjected him to a subtle and intensive campaign of selective information. They presented the PLO to Kreisky as a great humanitarian organisation, spending most of its wealth on hospitals, education and pensions for the Palestinian people. In fact, it does spend much money on such services for families associated with the PLO, though not for Palestinians generally. Kreisky, a humane man, was found to be a softsell for this approach and he became a great admirer of Arafat.

In September 1979 Arafat was publicly embraced in Madrid by the Spanish premier, Adolfo Suarez. While

Arafat was in Iberia, Farouk Khaddoumi in Rome accepted 'political recognition' from the Italian Foreign Minister, Franco Maria Malfatti. In Brussels, Khaddoumi held a joint press conference with the Foreign Minister, Henri Simonet, during which the Palestinian claimed de facto recognition from Belgium. Simonet did not challenge this interpretation of the meeting. 'It seems to us,' said Simonet, 'that the PLO is now the means and the vehicle through which the will of the Palestinian people is being expressed.'

While in Brussels Khaddoumi had yet another meeting, this time with Claude Cheysson, the European Commissioner in charge of relations with developing countries.

I witnessed an Arafat triumph in Portugal in November 1979 when he addressed a crowd of 10,000 in Lisbon's sports arena. 'In the name of every man, woman and child in Palestine,' he cried, 'to every child, woman and man, to every house, valley, every rock in Portugal, I say, thank you, thank you, thank you.' His presence there was the result of four years of constant and elaborate propaganda, financed by Libya. The occasion was a five-day 'World Conference in Support of the Arab People and Palestine,' which brought 750 delegates from 80 countries. Arafat was received as virtual head of state and had private audiences with the Premier, Maria de Lourdes Pintassiligo, the President, Antonio Ramalho Eanes, and the Socialist leader, Mario Soares. At a Press conference, Arafat said, 'Up until now the European countries accepted only the point of view of our enemies, but now we have the feeling that there has been a change.'

This parade of triumphs owed much to the Saudi Arabians. They had commended the PLO to the major European countries. A West German diplomat told *Time* magazine (November 19, 1979), 'When the Saudis quietly suggest that it makes sense to talk to the PLO you just don't dismiss it out of hand.'

Saudi influence may have been involved in the diplomatic recognition accorded the PLO by Senegal, Nepal and India during 1980. Mrs. Gandhi, that autocratic leader of the country with the world's second largest population who is sometimes 'unavailable' when Western diplomats wish to see her, personally waited on the runway at Delhi airport for Arafat's arrival. The Nicaraguan foreign minister, Tomas Borge, stated that the cause of the PLO is the cause of the Sandanistas. A PLO representative is said to have threatened Japan with numerous though unspecified dangers if the organisation were not to get diplomatic recognition in Tokyo. Since the PLO and the terrorist Japanese Red Army Faction have close links such threats were not to be taken lightly.

Regardless of any help from the Arab superpowers the PLO makes many of its own openings and creates opportunities for its leaders to be seen with Western statesmen and ambassadors. This was well shown in March 1980 when a party was held in Beirut to farewell the British Ambassador, Mr. Ben Strachan, on his return to London. The party was arranged by a leading PLO agent in Lebanon, Chafic al Hout, and to nobody's surprise Yasser Arafat turned up. It is difficult to know whether Mr. Strachan was 'set up,' whether he was naive in accepting the invitation or whether he simply supports the PLO. It was certainly unwise of him, as a senior diplomat, to attend any party organised by a political group.

PLO agents had worked since 1976 on the idea of opening an office in Dublin. Eire was desirable because of hints that it would support the 'European initiative'. Even more important, Eire had become a member of the UN Security Council and was therefore influential. On top of all this, in 1979 two Irish soldiers serving in the UN force in Lebanon had been killed and Israel had been blamed for their deaths. The Irish Government responded favourably to PLO overtures, once the PLO representative in London, Nabil Ramlawi, who conducted the negotiations, had declared that the PLO had no connection with the IRA. In fact it is well known in Intelligence circles that members of the IRA have had modern training, especially in explosives, in PLO camps in Lebanon. The Irish Government announced in March 1981 the opening of a PLO office but said that it would not be regarded as an 'official representation.' Since neither the PLO nor any other private organisation would need to seek government permission to set up an office it was significant that the Foreign Affairs Department felt constrained to make an announcement. Ramlawi was able to organise a group called 'Irish Friends of Palestine,' whose president at once announced that the opening of the office amounted to de facto recognition of the PLO.

The PLO central office is quick to seize an opportunity to establish itself in fresh regions. Such a chance came in July 1979 when Palestinian terrorists occupied the Egyptian Embassy in Ankara. A PLO negotiating team flew from Damascus to Ankara, entered the Egyptian Embassy and persuaded the terrorists to surrender peacefully to the Turkish authorities. In return Turkey authorised the PLO to open a permanent office in Ankara. It has since become clear that the PLO team made this deal before leaving Damascus and this suggests that the embassy take-over could have been planned for this very purpose. In October 1979 Arafat himself opened the new office in Ankara, and was welcomed by the premier of the time, Bulent Evecit.

Another PLO propaganda coup took place in Aberdeen. Palestinian agents induced a majority of the city's councillors to twin Aberdeen with Nablus, the principal Arab city on the West Bank and main base on the West Bank for PLO activities. Mr. Bassam Shak'a, major of Nablus, and a militant PLO supporter, presented the PLO flag to the council when he was invited to Aberdeen as a guest. It was placed in the entrance hall to the council chamber and was the source of much publicity for the PLO.

Even in Holland, where pro-Israeli sentiment is strong, support for the Palestinians has doubled, according to a poll. The great majority of the Dutch would like a Palestinian state though a majority is still against recognition of the PLO. Success in Holland has been due to Dutch academics, particularly at the University of Amsterdam, won over by PLO propaganda.

Significant propaganda is issued obliquely through the

United Nations Relief and Works Agency (UNRWA) whose mission is to care for Palestinian refugees in Lebanon and other countries. Indirectly, but no less effectively, UNRWA was 'taken over' by the PLO, through the Palestinians who work for UNWRA in Lebanon and to a lesser extent in other countries. At least until the Lebanon war of 1975-76 the Beirut headquarters of UNRWA was part of a major propaganda production and distribution operation and there is some evidence to suggest that it started up again in 1978. The regular publication *Palestinian Refugees Today* is as emotive as factual and unauthorised sheets are sometimes slipped between its pages. Other writers and I have gained entry to Palestinian camps which have terrorist training centres more readily through UNRWA contacts than through PLO public relations channels. Some Palestinian employees of UNRWA pass to Fatah, as a routine, any reports of Israeli troop movements gleaned by UN workers. In 1977 the prominent US senator Jacob Javitts sent an aide, Hal Rosenthal, to the Middle East to investigate the alleged diversion of UNRWA funds to the PLO; Rosenthal was killed in a terrorist attack on an El Al plane at Istanbul airport on August 15 and this murder may have been arranged by the PLO to prevent any investigation from taking place.

PLO propaganda tactics have been nowhere more successful than those used to influence the United Nations Interim Force in Lebanon—UNIFIL—sent to southern Lebanon in 1976. In less than a year the PLO had infiltrated it to such an extent that, for all practical purposes, it controlled UNIFIL.

For instance, it had induced UNIFIL to hire Arab terrorists to guard its base headquarters in Beirut. Soon after this UNIFIL supplied the PLO commander in southern Lebanon, which technically is UNIFIL territory, with ultra-sophisticated communications equipment. PLO liaison officers were allowed to move at will around UNIFIL territory fully armed and with an armed escort. Regular encampments of PLO forces were allowed to remain intact within UNIFIL territory and UNIFIL supplied them with food and equipment.

PLO propaganda induced individual UNIFIL officers to smuggle explosives into Israel for use by PLO terrorists. UNIFIL commanders also undertook to return to the PLO within 24 hours any of their men captured while carrying out illegal military activities in UNIFIL territory. Their weapons are returned within a week.

The PLO quickly persuaded UNIFIL officers to inform village mukhtars or leaders and PLO liaison officers 24 hours in advance of any impending search for concealed weapons. These searches thus were useless. From the Israelis' point of view the worst breach of UNIFIL impartiality was to instigate reports that the Israelis, after killing five terrorists, dynamited and otherwise mutilated their bodies. These reports had world wide publicity. A UN board of inquiry carried out a post-mortem which established that the wounds were 'normal battle wounds.' UNIFIL did not publicise this correction. In November 1980 UNIFIL records did mention 90 PLO-provoked incidents in UNIFIL territory but these figures were given little publicity. In December UNIFIL and the PLO reached an agreement about co-operation in southern Lebanon but the number of PLO-provoked incidents rose to 140, also little publicised.

UNIFIL has never achieved any real degree of authority in its designated area. It has no control in the town of Tyre, which is ruled by the PLO, and no control of the 'buffer zone' along Israel's northern border, which is administered by a private Christian-Muslim army under Major Saad Haddad. UNIFIL has not been able to check persistent PLO infiltration into and right through its area of occupation. In fairness, the United Nations force, armed with nothing more effective than light mortars, has never had the military force to compel compliance with its orders.

Another type of propaganda triumph in 1976 was the invitation to the PLO, with eight other 'liberation' groups, to attend the UN Habitat Conference in Vancouver. Even more significant was the PLO's participation in the International Air Transport Association's conference on air safety. The main matter for discussion was prevention of hijacking—at a time when PLO groups were active in hijacking. I was a guest at a Palestinian social gathering in Nablus, on the West Bank, when the PLO's participation in this IATA conference was announced over the radio; the reaction was one of bemused astonishment. At the time the IATA connection was regarded as 'the ultimate' in propaganda achievement.

A major more abstract propaganda victory has been propagation of the idea that the 'Palestinian issue' is the major threat to peace in the Middle East. Linked with this is the secondary motion that the Palestinian affair is closely bound up with the 'oil issue.' If the first problem could be solved, PLO propaganda has insisted, a solution to the second must follow. Arafat himself uses the slogan, 'The two Ps—petroleum and Palestine.' This presentation is so insistently preached that politicians in many countries have come to produce it as their own idea. This then permits the PLO propagandists to quote Europeans, Africans, Americans and others as having made the statement; thus, the principle of black propaganda—that its true origin be concealed—is fulfilled. The success of this particular propaganda plot was evident when the Palestinian and oil issues were linked in speeches made by Chancellor Kreisky and even more satisfying to the PLO when the EEC leaders, at their Venice meeting, referred to the 'Palestinian issue' as the principal threat to Middle East peace.

This is demonstrably not so. At no time since 1948 has the Middle East had less then a score of dangerously explosive inter-Arab, or inter-Muslim conflicts, and even more internal disputes. The Iraqi-Iranian war which began in 1980 was only one of the more spectacular disturbances. The more or less permanent conflicts include Saudi Arabia v South Yemen; Iran v United Arab Emirates; Oman v UAE and South Yemen; South Yemen v

Yemen and Somalia; Libya v Sudan, Egypt and Tunisia; Algeria v Morocco.

The Middle East is also the confrontation site for the superpowers. Any one of many factors is potentially more dangerous than the Palestinian issue—or even the Arab-Israeli issue. The precarious internal condition of the majority of the regimes in which the West has traditionally placed its economic and political trust are also more dangerous than the 'Palestine issue.' Libya and Iran were considered pillars of stability but they fell, and in both cases to extremists bent on spreading revolution. Saudi Arabia is intrinsically unstable with its oil-based economy, a feudal society, a population of over 30 per cent foreigners and a large Shi'a minority in the oil provinces. Bahrein, Kuwait and Oman, again with large Shi'a minorities, are also fundamentally unstable and could be flashpoints for war. Iraq is a powder keg waiting to blow up. Its Sunni minority of 25 per cent dominates a Shi'a majority of 50 per cent and militant Turkoman and Kurdish minorities are ceaselessly rebellious. Communist elements oppose the central government, which is further weakened by the unwillingness of the Iraqi tribal masses to support any centralised regime. Between 1936 and 1973 Iraq suffered from one coup d'etat after another and in July 1979 100,000 Shi'a people were killed outright or judicially executed by President Saddam Hussein after an abortive revolution.

None of these confrontations has any relationship to the Palestinian issue.

The propaganda that a solution to the Palestinian problem is connected to the flow of oil to the West has some substance, but more as a threat than as a weapon. Oil prices and supplies have been much more affected by the national interests of each individual oil-producing state than by OPEC dictates. The Iran–Iraq war menaced the West's oil supplies, if only because 70 per cent of OPEC's oil passes through the Straits of Hormuz, which could be closed if the war were to reach a critical stage. This danger is in no way related to the Palestinian question.

It does not seem credible that Saudi Arabia, whose oil constitutes 90 per cent of her exports, should sacrifice herself by withholding oil production in the name of a nebulous Palestinian ideal, the achievement of which it can seek in other ways. The Palestinians were not mentioned during the OPEC meeting in Geneva in May 1981; members were more worried about the oil glut in the West and ways of overcoming it.

In the United States the Arab propagandists know that they will have won a battle if they can neutralise the influential Jewish lobbies, particularly in Washington and New York. For this, if for no other reason, Arab public relations experts have supported overtly anti-semitic organisations. The Arab campaign in the US involves more than 100 fulltime American professionals—experts in advertising, public affairs, communications and political lobbying. It is believed that in 1981 the Arab propaganda campaign had a budget of about £20 million and that perhaps half of this was spent by the PLO.

During the Carter administration, an American public relations expert produced a propaganda and publicity credo for the PLO, with special attention to the United States. Its thesis is that 'the war will be won not on the battlefield, nor even around the conference table, so much as in the minds of Americans.'

The document is concerned mainly with 'a good image' in the United States, to which end the PLO should 'coalesce' with opposition political groups in Israel as a means of showing that the PLO is not flatly opposed to talking with Israelis. The credo advises Arafat to study television techniques, from facial expressions to gestures and verbal responses. PLO lobbyists in Washington should copy Jewish methods, and, the document states, Arab propagandists generally should 'take away Jewish control of the [Middle East] debate.' John Richardson, a prominent member of the National Association for Arab Americans, is quoted as saying that 'rather then be pro-Arab be pro-American.'

The credo suggests that the arena of conflict between

Israel and the PLO moved to the US during the days of the Nixon Doctrine, when the American State Department began to view the Middle East conflict as a regional one, and no longer only in terms of the Arabs and Jews.

The author of the study suggests that the PLO align itself with the American black community. Noting that the American black is 'deeply religious,' he recommends stress in propaganda on 'the role of the Christians in the Palestinian elite.'

[It is true that many upper-class Palestinians are Christians but only a few PLO leaders are Christian; George Habash is one.]

In exploitation of the Christian connection, Americans should be told that 'the Vatican does not recognise Israel.' [It does but, as Farouk Khaddoumi's reception by Cardinal Casaroli shows, there is a significant Vatican anti-Israel lobby.]

The American analyst urges Arafat to engage professional speechwriters, especially when he is to appear before Western audiences. The PLO should also concentrate, in its publicity, on the stories of Palestinian children and old people; 'the American public is far less sympathetic to the plight of people in the prime of life.'

The document places heavy emphasis on techniques and the PLO is urged not to buy paid advertisements, 'as only the Federal Bureau of Investigation reads them.' Propagandists should also 'go easy' on Sadat, as he is popular in the United States. 'It would be better to describe his treaty with Israel more in sorrow than in anger.' On relations with the American press, the expert cautions the PLO to avoid contact with publishers and editors, if only because 'the United States is not Cairo' where such people are influential. The truly influential in America are 'the top news personalities,' who have the authority to decide what stories to cover.

That the Press propaganda was having some success can be seen by a frontpage headline in the *Christian Science Monitor* of August 6, 1979: THE PLO'S NEW NICE-

GUY IMAGE. The support heading reads: *On several fronts the PLO seems to be softening towards Israel.*

The PLO is advised to concentrate on those states of the US with smaller populations 'where the Zionist lobby is weak.' The expert states: 'It would do no harm for Arafat to explain the tightrope he has to walk to keep majority PLO support behind him,' to emphasise that if he fails in his aims the desperate minority will take more violent action.

The report suggests making odious comparisons between the West Bank under Israeli military administration and the Bantustans of South Africa, and between Jewish settlers in the administered territories and 'red-neck' colonialists. PLO propagandists should also compare the Israeli military administration with 'military occupations' elsewhere in the world.

The PLO plan to win the Christian churches of the United States to its cause had begun early in the 1970s. Almost unnoticed by the news media a growing number of churches began to show interest in the Middle East and then to focus attention on the PLO. In many cases the change was gradual but the trend was reinforced by debate over Andrew Young's unauthorised contact with a representative of the PLO when Young was UN ambassador, an action that cost Young his job.

Most of the church groups that have come out in support of Palestinian rights have been careful to emphasise that they advocate as well—in keeping with the United Nations resolutions on the subject—the right of Israel to exist within secure borders. This is true of the National Council of Churches, an organisation representing 31 Protestant and orthodox denominations, which made the year 1979-80 a 'focus of study', as requested by the PLO literature they had been receiving. The council's executive commended Ambassador Young for talking with the PLO representative—again as urged by the PLO.

In keeping with the theme of Middle East study, the Presbyterian Church in the United States listened to several Palestinian speakers at a conference in North

Carolina in July 1979. Richard Butler, director of the Middle East office of the National Council of Churches, has said, 'There is an increased understanding of the centrality of the Palestinian issue in the Middle East conflict. Many churches have dealt for years with the Palestinian issue as a refugee problem. Only recently have they come to recognise that the Palestinians are not just refugees. They are a people looking for a homeland.'

Butler's phraseology faithfully reflects PLO literature; the slogans 'people looking for a homeland' and 'centrality of the Palestinian issue' are the key phrases suggested by one of the public relations firms engaged by the PLO to present its case to the Americans.

The PLO has had great success in presenting itself as a 'liberation' or 'resistance' movement. The theme of liberation is popular in the Third World, while 'resistance' appeals to the Europeans because of their memories of the Nazi invaders. In PLO literature comparisons are frequent with the European underground movements that harassed the Nazis during World War II. Guerrilla-type actions inside Israel and the administered territories are described as 'the spontaneous acts of any people resisting occupation.'

In the Third World and in any country which once was part of an Empire the PLO speaks of the Israelis as 'imperialists' and 'colonialists', if not in their own right then as agents for the United States. The Israeli agronomists who were helping undeveloped countries were really 'the agents of imperialism' bent on exploitation of these countries' natural resources. The campaign was strikingly effective—in the mid 1970s most of the Third World countries expelled their Israeli helpers and in many cases broke off diplomatic relations.

The practical methods by which the PLO puts its propaganda strategy into practice fall into seven fairly precise categories—repetition of slogans; dramatic impact from carefully posed and sometimes faked photographs; large advertisements in leading newspapers; exploitation of Western, and especially American, anxieties through interviews with leading PLO men; use of Palestinian academics and their work to give the PLO a respectable face; maintenance of a steady stream of newspapers, magazines, leaflets and posters and radio programmes;* arousal of sympathy through human interest stories circulated to the media.

There is nothing new in any of these tactics; the great use-of-propaganda nations—Britain, France, Germany, the Soviet Union and the United States—have exploited all of them many times. But the PLO propagandists have achieved a degree of professionalism unequalled in the 20th century except perhaps by the American propaganda machine in World War I in selling the war to its own people, and by the Nazis in deluding Europe before World War II into believing that they were not militarists.

I have referred already to some of the basic slogans. Others are 'No peace without the Palestinians,' 'Muslims, Christians and Jews united,' 'Dare you fly El Al?' (a PFLP slogan in the heyday of hijacking.) 'Revolution Until Victory;' 'Long live an Arab Free Palestine,' 'Palestinian entity.' 'Justice and peace come from the cannon's mouth' —the Mao doctrine; 'Building up the fighting party, every fighter a politician, every politician a fighter' (PFLP); 'Fatah's fighters specialise in the art of death for the sake of life.' 'We are all commandos', 'Drive the Israelis into the sea,' 'Fatah, fatherland, Arafat.'

Slogans are ephemeral and their usefulness depends on the political situation. The label-slogan 'Black September' came into use as a name for the period when King Hussein drove the Palestinian terrorists from Jordan. The slogan which has had most currency abroad is 'A lay democratic, pluralistic Palestine'—or a version of this—which for several years convinced many Europeans that the PLO really believed that Arabs and Jews could live in amity,

---

* In mid-1980 the PLO launched propaganda directly into Israel through a Hebrew-language radio programme on the PLO *Voice of Palestine*.

intermingled, on the one piece of land. 'The international Zionist conspiracy' was a slogan much used during the 1960s and part of the 1970s; because it has been discredited it is now used only by the radical left of the PLO—in common with the National Front type organisation of the Western world.

Brilliant propaganda photographs abound, many of them taken by the professionals employed by UNWRA. The best of them show refugees—the elderly man with grizzled face and fathomless eyes, the little girl with large round eyes eating a piece of bread and jam with flies on it, the woman weeping for her son killed in a raid across the Israeli border, the family in their austere hut, the over-large class of eager school children. . . . These photographs are genuine but the sharp, posed focus upon despair, hunger, longing and hardship and all the other human feelings is intended to rouse pity for the Palestinians and anger against the Israelis, who are depicted as having caused all these miseries.

Faked photographs are unusually exploited in outright attacks on Israel, and most of them emanate from the occupied territories. One of the most-used fakes is that which shows an Arab woman in a Gaza street apparently under arrest by two Israeli soldiers carrying Uzi machineguns. In fact, the figure of the woman has been superimposed on the original print of two patrolling soldiers. In another photograph an elderly Arab woman is shown apparently holding up her hands in surrender to a scowling Israeli soldier; the lady is, in fact, walking along in a prayer posture and the Israeli's features have been touched up to make them black and unfriendly. A third photograph shows about sixteen Arab schoolgirls walking along a street towards an Israeli soldier standing in a menacing position with a machine-gun; in fact, it was his regular job to protect the girls against grenade-throwing terrorists on their way to school. The producers of fake photographs generally do not use captions and rely on a picture to tell its own story, a propaganda subtlety never used by the

Nazis, who relied on exaggerated messages which accompanied their photographs.

The PLO leans heavily on warnings and threats against the West. For instance, in an open letter published in the *Washington Post* and *New York Times*—as a paid advertisement—there is more than a hint of moral blackmail. 'It is not in your interest to alienate millions of Arabs, Moslems and Afro-Asians. . . . It is not in your interest to continue to spend billions of dollars in perpetuation of Zionist dreams of empire. It is not in your interest to re-activate the energy crisis.'

Arafat himself is the PLO's expert on appeals to Americans' self-interest, and being the most-interviewed international figure in *Time* Magazine between 1970 and 1980 he has had plenty of opportunities. On February 11, 1980 Arafat made these observations;

On US military power in the Middle East:
'You cannot use Israel as your spearhead for bases. That is impossible. Israel has been a burden to you in the past, but now it is becoming a great burden. If you try to use Israel as your base in this area, the reaction will be too much. I am not talking of Arab reaction but of *Muslim* reaction. You know how great that Muslim reaction is. If you try to use those bases you will lose everything. You asked the Muslims to come together against the Soviets, but they will also be together against you.'

On the US and the PLO: 'I used to be a civil engineer. I know a little mathematics. In calculus there is the odd number. A differential equation has an odd number, and without that number there is no solution to the equation. You are at a crucial moment in your history. Why, at this most crucial moment, do you neglect the Palestinians, who are the odd number in the Middle East? If you recognise Palestine, then the whole equation of the Muslim world will work for you. The problem will be solved. Why can't your computers tell you this?'

On American policy towards Israel: 'When American interests are endangered, you have to talk about practical steps in dealing with Israel. Without an independent Palestinian state, the Americans cannot convince the Arab states, or the Palestinians, to accept Camp David or Egypt or to go along with your policy in this part of the world.'

The PLO leadership early realised that its own Research Centre would quickly be seen as a propaganda factory so the Institute for Palestine Studies was founded at a different Beirut address and under academic management. Its director, Walid Khadduri, an Iraqi, with specialist training in publicity and propaganda, was instructed to make the Institute prestigious. One step was to produce the *Journal of Palestine Studies*, sub-titled 'A quarterly on Palestinian affairs and the Arab-Israeli conflict.' To lend it greater academic weight on the cover appeared 'Published jointly by the Institute for Palestine Studies and Kuwait University.' In fact, Kuwait's contribution was solely a financial one.

The Institute appointed as editor a distinguished American-Palestinian scholar, Dr. Hisham Sharabi, and gave him an editorial board of other notable Palestinian professors and specialists in various fields. The first issue was published in Autumn 1971 and was impressive in its contents. In his first editorial, Sharabi wrote: 'This journal addresses itself to an international audience. . . . It focuses on a global conflict; a conflict which, though engaging a relatively small number of people over a relatively small extent of territory, leads the greatest powers on earth into a confrontation threatening the peace and security of the whole world. . . . The Journal . . . will not engage in polemics or become a propaganda vehicle. Commitment does not preclude fairness or objectivity. We believe that the cause of peace and justice in Palestine is best served by adhering to the facts and their unbiased analysis.'

The contents list of the first issue makes interesting reading and is representative of later issues:

War and peace in the Middle East—in an interview with Mohammad Hassanein Heykal, then editor of Cairo's *Al-Ahram*; Israel's nuclear options, by Fuad Jabber; The Middle East conflict in US Strategy 1970-71, by William Quandt; Recent Knesset Legislation and the Arabs in Israel by Sabri Jiryis, a staff member of the Institute; University students in Lebanon and the Palestinian Resistance, by Halim Barakat, a professor at the American University of Beirut; The fall of Jerusalem, 1967 by Abdullah Schleiffer. A good half of the Journal was taken up with political happenings of the quarter, reviews of books and periodicals and discussion of documents and source material.

Despite Dr. Sharabi's claim for impartiality, the Journal is a propaganda vehicle, though at a discreet and intellectual level; it relies for its effect on the reputation and authority of its editor and contributors. Its readers are other academics, writers and researchers of various nationalitites, and few could be unimpressed with its professionalism. It never openly praises the PLO or any of its constituent bodies but recounts their activities in terse, note form; the first issue lists 41 pamphlets by Fatah in Arabic, 11 in English and 4 in French, and all other papers brought out by all the 'commando' organisations. This gives both the organisations and their pamphlets a large degree of respectability, as it was designed to do.

Whatever the front presented by propaganda—the 'nice-guy' image, moderation, the PLO as the true voice of the Palestinian people—veteran observers have learned that truth is more likely to be found in what PLO spokesmen say to their own people in Arabic; they then feel secure from quotation in the foreign media.

Two statements stand out as particularly significant.

'The Palestinian resistance will make no concessions in the future, and it will grant no recognition to the existing Zionist entity.' Khaled al-Hassan, political adviser to Yasser Arafat, speaking at a meeting of the Euro-Arab Parliamentary Association December 14, 1980, as quoted in *Al-Madina al-Munawara*, Riyadh, December 15.

'Machine guns and rifle bullets are the only way to reach an understanding with the Zionist enemy. Statements, protests and UN resolutions are of no avail, only the massive use of bullets. . . . Our people cannot cease its struggle, which is carried out with bullets, machine guns and hand grenades.' Khalil Al-Wazir (Abu Jihad) Chief of Fatah and one of the three most important PLO leaders, as quoted by *Voice of Palestine*, Beirut, May 3, 1980.

Chapter Six

The European Connection

On March 18, 1981 in the House of Commons, Winston Churchill MP put a question—during Oral Answers to Questions on Foreign and Commonwealth Affairs—to the Deputy Foreign Secretary, Sir Ian Gilmour:

'What grounds can my right honourable friend advance for believing that the PLO is any more representative of the wishes and aspirations of the Palestinian people than the IRA is of the Irish Catholic community in Northern Ireland?'

Gilmour's reply: 'I do not think that my honourable friend can be serious in asking that question. . . . It has often been shown, both in the Republic of Ireland and in the North, that the IRA enjoys virtually no popular support. If my honourable friend believes that the PLO enjoys no popular support among the Palestinians, either on the West Bank, in the refugee camps or elsewhere, he should go there and find out for himself.'

A month later Robert Sands, an IRA criminal gaoled in the Maze prison, won the by-election in Fermanagh —South Tyrone with a majority of 1,446 votes over the former leader of the Official Unionist Party (Protestant). Sands' victory (he later committed suicide by starvation) was considered a notable triumph for the IRA; it was thus proved that the IRA did represent Catholics in Northern Ireland, and Israel's friends were quick to ask if the British Government would now recognise the IRA and negotiate with them, just as they were pressing Israel to do with the PLO.

Sir Ian's belief that the PLO has popular support among Palestinians is partly based on the single most important piece of propaganda concerning the PLO—that it has strong 'moderate' elements. Interestingly, this evaluation was propagated by Westerners, though the Soviet Union has also presented Arafat as a moderate. One might with some cynical realism suggest that when the Soviet goes out of its way to declare somebody a moderate he is anything but that.

The word 'moderate' is not used by the Arabs and was certainly not used by the PLO before it was put forward in the West, perhaps by people who had a strong desire to *see* moderation; Western governments, frustrated and exasperated by the unending Middle East conflict, naturally grasp at the slightest indication of moderation. Having perceived this desire, and having evaluated it as a weakness, PLO propaganda has exploited it, as have the official propagandists of several Arab nations.

If proof were needed of the continuing uncompromising Arab attitude to Israel, even among 'moderate' states, it was contained in the official Jordanian declaration at the end of the visit to Amman in 1981 by the US Secretary of State Alexander Haig. It was a reiteration of the usual formula—that a just and lasting peace in the Middle East could be achieved only on the basis of total Israeli withdrawal from all the territories occupied after the 1967 war, the restoration of Palestinian rights and recognition of the PLO as the legitimate representative of the Palestinian people.

President Sadat's visit to Israel in November 1977 had showed that the PLO and its supporters had no moderate element. From the moment of Sadat's arrival the PLO consistently rejected all attempts at compromise with Israel. Indeed, there had been little willingness to compromise before that. Interviewed by *Newsweek* on March 3, 1977, Farouk Khaddoumi, having advocated moderation, explained what he meant: 'We mean . . . we are ready to

74

establish a state on part of our territory. In the past we said no, it had to be on all of it, immediately, a democratic state of Palestine. Now we say this can be implemented in stages. That's moderation.' After the Sadat visit to Israel Khaddoumi intimated that he might accept Palestinian sovereignty within a part of Israel as 'a preliminary stage.' The rejectionists consistently maintain that the PLO goal must be pursued without any initial compromise. The difference between the rejectionists and those described as moderates appears to be only one of means to the same end.

Robert Mabro of the Centre of Middle Eastern Studies, Oxford, has said that Arafat is posing as a broker. 'He is setting himself up as an intermediary, saying that he has leverage in some places, but he cannot make any huge promises. In the meantime, European countries can give him something diplomatic, like an office. That way he can advance step by step.'*

Whatever the diplomatic niceties extended to the PLO they have failed to shield Western Europe from oil price rises. Although France played an important role in moving its European partners closer to Arafat, the French were not particularly successful in developing privileged relations with the oil-producing states of the Middle East.

European interest in the Middle East conflict stems largely from political and economic vulnerability. But the European statesmen have apparently not thought the dilemma through to a logical conclusion. They have selected a policy which, if successful, would make a war more likely rather than less likely. They favour a PLO state which would be anything but an agent of stability in the region. There is an attractive vision as an end product of satisfying Arab demands—oil would become cheap and its supply 'safe'; the Soviet would not get a foothold in the area as the Arabs would be friendly to the West; Western business interests would prosper in the Arab world and Western military bases would then be possible.

*_Time_ Magazine, November 19,1979

The EEC countries need oil and strive to ingratiate themselves with the Arab world. They know of the £130,000 million of Arab money waiting to be spent. Much of this is on deposit or invested short-term but a great deal more money can be made in selling arms to the Middle East countries. The scope of this market is so tremendous that it over-rides moral, political and intellectual arguments. The biggest and best customer is Saudi Arabia, taking about half of total Western arms shipped into the Middle East. The US supplies much of this material but France signed a single £1,600 million arms deal in May 1980. Even before this it had supplied 1000 AMX tanks—which equals the tank strength of the French Army. In 1981 there were 450 French military advisers in Saudi Arabia, some involved with the £1,000 million air-defence missile complex and others in training Saudis to fly France's Mirage 4000. Austria sells anti-aircraft and machine-guns. Britain sold 'support equipment for artillery' worth £130 million in one deal, as well as patrol boats, tanks and aircraft. Switzerland and Italy in collaboration provided Saudi Arabia with a £1,300 million air-defence system. West Germany in 1981 sold Saudi Arabia patrol boats and training ships. Also, the Germans sold to Syria tanks, armoured cars and ancillary equipment. French arms deals with Iraq amount to £1,000 million a year for the six years 1980-1986. Spain, too, in 1980 concluded a five-year agreement with Iraq for arms worth £500 million. These are just a few examples of the vast amounts of money being spent in the West; Libya, for instance, spends £2,000 million a year. Behind all the deals is the tacit understanding that Europe will 'do what it can' for the PLO.

The short-term advantages are obvious—greater prosperity for the West at a time of recession. But in the long-term, quite apart from any Arab-Israel confrontation, great dangers exist. The huge supply of arms puts added power into the hands of armed forces which are often the enemies of social progress and the biggest barriers of all to democratic government. The more arms are poured into the Middle East the more likely it is that the West will be forced into intervention in regional conflicts which become an unbearable threat to Western interests.

Apart from this, powerful forces within the Arab world are making the whole region more militantly Islamic and turning it against the West to begin a new era of Islamic revival; the ultimate aim is Islamic domination, as expressed by Gaddafi.

Beyond the purely economic advantages of being co-operative with the Arab states about the PLO are European personal and nationalistic ambitions and needs. For instance, in receiving Arafat in July 1979, Bruno Kreisky, Chancellor of Austria, was furthering his ambition to carve a greater international role for his small, neutral, pro-Western republic and enhancing his own image as a world statesman.*

Giscard d'Estaing proposed 'self-determination' for the Palestinians for his own reasons and a perceptive *Guardian* reporter perceived them. 'He has shown his characteristically adroit sense of timing in making his well publicised announcement in Kuwait . . . He knows it will do France no harm in the Arab world to be seen pioneering the European Community's way towards supporting self-determination for the Palestinians.'

For Chancellor Schmidt, too, 'Palestinian self-determination' makes some sense. He believes that his Palestinian policy fits into his policy of détente with the Soviet Union and solidarity within the EEC with France.

Spain's motives in issuing an official invitation to Arafat were transparent; the country could not survive without Arab oil. Much of this oil comes from Libya and Algeria, both of which had urged the Spanish Government to invite Arafat. His presence there, and his hardline comments

---

* While the Kreisky-Brandt-Arafat talks were in progress a PLO squad was intercepted on its way to Israel from south Lebanon. Its mission was to seize civilian hostages. Also, at that moment dozens of researchers, politicians and journalists from around the world were convening in Jerusalem to discuss ways of combating terror, the emphasis being on PLO involvement in international terrorism.

concerning Israel, caused great distress in Israel. A spokesman for the Israeli Foreign Ministry said that given the total absence of any diplomatic relations between the two countries and the non-recognition of the existence of Israel by Spain, Israel could express no official reaction. Nevertheless, officials were shocked that Spain, whose return to the fold of the Western-style democracies had been so warmly welcomed by Jerusalem, had chosen to give such an open welcome to the leader of the PLO. In fact, the PLO had beaten Israel to the initiative: Spain had announced major cultural exchanges between itself and Israel and the PLO central bureau wanted to sabotage them, hence the angling for a State invitation.

The 'European initiative,' articulated at the Venice summit in June 1980, had four main thrusts. First, it declared that 'the Palestinian people must be placed in a position to exercise fully their right to self-determination.' It also asserted that the PLO 'will have to be associated' with any peace settlement. Further, it called for the creation of a European fact-finding mission, probably of Cabinet-level membership, to determine the position of the adversaries and explore new avenues of negotiation. Finally, even though it upheld Israel's unquestioned 'right to secure borders' it sharply criticised Israel for establishing settlements on the West Bank, a process it called 'a serious obstacle to peace.'

The European leaders expressed their desire to bring the PLO into the 'peace-making process' just two weeks after the PLO had once more stated its intention of liquidating Israel. They made concessions to the PLO in advance with the result that the PLO would not after that see any reason to make concessions in return.

The Venice Summit was the starting point for the mission by Gaston Thorn, Luxembourg's Foreign Minister and then president of the Conference of Foreign Ministers, to search for an opening for the European initiative. That he found one was clear in November 1980 when the EEC took a long step towards formally recognising the PLO. EEC officials had two days of talks with an

Arab team led by Ahmed Sedki al-Dajani, a member of the PLO executive. The PLO at once used this as evidence for claiming that the EEC is increasingly ready to recognise the PLO as a legitimate factor in Middle-East diplomacy.

In fact, on the European side it is the Parliamentary Association for Euro-Arab Cooperation rather than the EEC governments, which makes the running. This association is a straightforward pressure group, more concerned with Europe getting on with the Arabs than with the Arabs and the Israelis getting on with each other.

Europe's official policy begins from a faulty and obsolete premise—that its role is to help clarify whether a Palestinian entity should be created in the administered territories. Its real role is in clarifying *how* it will take shape. But Europe's only strong card is its freedom to talk to the PLO — a liberty which the United States has denied itself. The only way that Europe can operate effectively is through the US, with all its influence on Israel. The Europeans must work with the Americans—if not alongside them, then in the same direction. But Europe has a major problem, to establish its good faith—which is not accepted in Israel and in some quarters in America—and its practical efficiency as a working partner in a complex situation.

Absence of good faith and lack of efficiency was seen by the Americans (and by the Israelis) when Willy Brandt, in Vienna for another meeting, accepted Kreisky's invitation to meet Arafat. Brandt, noted more for idealism than political adroitness, accepted, creating embarrassment in Bonn; the West German government dissociated itself from Brandt's action. Later a visibly startled Brandt appeared to comprehend the implications of his participation. 'None of my friends in Israel should think that my loyalty to them is in any way diminished,' he said. It was fairly clear that this was *not* the Israelis main reaction; what alarmed them was the political ineptitude of a leading Western European statesman and the probability that others would be equally inept.

The London *Guardian* considers that Europe has a small but important role, 'to stand in relation to the Palestinians as the Americans stand in relation to the Israelis: as their protector and guarantor.' The Palestinians are certainly in need of such protection, and as much from the PLO as from those Israelis who advocate expansionism. It is unfortunate for the Palestinians as much as for others that some Western leaders undermine the Camp David agreements and urge 'Palestinian self-determination' in isolation from the question of association between Palestinians and Jordanians, nearly 80 per cent of whom are themselves Palestinian.

European nations could do better than offer a 'school' solution to the Palestinian problem; they would be better advised to produce discussion papers. Also, they could use their 'recognition' of the PLO as a bargaining-counter instead of granting PLO demands in advance of negotiations.

The Europeans above all should consult President Mubarrak. President Mubarrak has also adopted this attitude. In a visit to Luxembourg in February 1981 President Sadat refrained from mentioning the PLO and later stated that this omission was deliberate. He would, he said, support the Palestinian people but not the self-appointed leaders of the PLO.

For the Palestinians a measure of protection, progress and self-determination might well have come out of Camp David. An American observer, writing in March 1981, impatiently chided the Europeans for their unwelcome interference. 'Camp David is by no means dead or even moribund. The alternative which the European initiative purports to offer is not only unrealistic but also a hindrance. So far as the EEC is concerned its members could play an honourable and constructive role were they to encourage the Arabs to sit at the negotiating table and the PLO to lay aside its grenades and guns. Such a policy might not ingratiate them with those who wield the oil weapon but it is more likely to contribute to peace than a policy of appeasement.'*

* William Frankel, *Christian Science Monitor*, March 6, 1981

80

British Government spokesmen throughout 1979-1981 stressed that the PLO had really become moderate—in ways which were never specified. The belief is bolstered by the repetition of pleasant-sounding theories—such as, the PLO was never really terrorist, that it is essentially a political grouping and that its leaders would be content with a mini-State. Such theories take no account of the unchanging Palestine National Covenant. The British appear to be the most naive of all the Europeans, perhaps because they accept Arab rhetoric—a natural part of Arab verbal presentation—at face value.

This could well have been the case with the British Liberal Party six-man delegation which studied the Arab-Israeli dispute late in 1980. It was headed by the party's leader David Steel and three members had long-standing pro-Palestinian leanings, even if not anti-Israeli ones.

The long report which followed the visit—which itself lasted only a few days—was confused and showed no understanding of the complexities of the problem. It revolved around certain assumptions made by the Liberals. These are the most significant: Israel has no need to 'fear a small fledgling Palestinian state' and 'any terrorism could be quickly isolated and denied any firm operating base.' These observations are also quotations from PLO propaganda.

Steel said that the PLO should be associated with any Middle East negotiations. His well-meant suggestion included no reference as to how the PLO could be made acceptable to the Israelis.

In January 1981 a delegation of British MPs—five Conservative and four Labour—visited Beirut to hold talks with PLO leaders. Arafat told them, 'Europe has a role and a responsibility towards international peace and security, but that role cannot be carried out as long as Europe is unable to free its will from US decisions on international issues, including the Palestinian question.' Arafat did not then believe that the policies of Shimon Peres differ from those of Menachem Begin. He told the

British MPs, 'Both men raise the slogan of exterminating the Palestinian people.'*

There has been no such slogan and no such policy; no Israeli government could survive nationally or internationally with this slogan. It has never been mentioned by any Western journalist, but the MPs appeared to believe Arafat and did not check his assertion.

The so-called Carrington policy, which demands 'self-determination' without regard for the consequences, has been described as 'not statesmanship but suicide.' A parallel would be Neville Chamberlain's policy of appeasement with Hitler in 1938-39. The Carrington policy is that of putting the short term benefits before the inevitable penalties of the year after next. Professor Walter Laquer has said (In *The New Republic*, March 7, 1981) 'It is a sad spectacle to watch the representatives of once great nations propounding the benefits of shortsightedness and irresponsible action and asking Americans to follow their example.' It was indeed very difficult to explain to Lord Carrington where his nation's best interests lie, though the Hon. T.C.F. Prittie, the veteran editor of the news-sheet, *Britain and Israel*, has tried. A letter written by Carrington to Prittie is full of significant statements and, together with Prittie's analysis, it makes interesting reading.

Carrington: 'In working for compromise, we must talk to all the parties, including the PLO whom, like it or not, most Palestinians regard as representing their views.'
Comment: The claim is debatable. Since no alternative Palestinian leadership has been allowed to come into being it is not possible to know whether 'most' Palestinians would accept the PLO's views. The PLO is an armed force and therefore it discourages more moderate views.
Carrington: 'If we are to make any progress towards peace we must try to influence the policies of the PLO.'
Comment: Such an approach is a proven failure; many European government leaders have not been able to

* *The Palestine Report*, No. 13, February 1981, produced by the London office of the PLO

induce the PLO to change its stated policy about the destruction of Israel.

Carrington: 'We have no illusions about the PLO.'

Comment: If this were so the Carrington policy would be radically different. Earlier Lord Carrington himself had said that he had no evidence to suggest that the PLO was a terrorist organisation. Murders and mass-murders by the score, claimed by the PLO, are evidence. A common illusion is that other terrorist groups, such as the PLP and PFLP, are not connected with the PLO. They are constituent parts of the PLO, with the right to participate in its funds.

Carrington: 'I do not accept the parallel between the PLO and the IRA.'

Comment: An attempt to draw a parallel might be unfair to the IRA. The IRA has, on the whole, struck at 'military' or 'official' targets, such as policemen or prison warders. The PLO strikes mainly at soft targets, such as women and children in kibbutzim. The PLO has also killed many more Arabs than Israelis. During one period, 1967-1972, the PLO in Gaza killed 49 Israeli soldiers and civilians and injured another 218. They killed 312 Arabs and injured 1,202; 50 children were among the dead and 260 children were wounded.

Carrington: 'The achievements of Camp David are remarkable but further progress towards a comprehensive settlement along that route looks unlikely.'

Comment: If the achievements are remarkable, as indeed they are, then this is reason enough to press on with Camp David; no other initiative can boast of so much success. A search for a 'comprehensive settlement' was bound to be a long one and to say that further progress 'looks unlikely' after only a few years is to surrender prematurely.

Carrington: 'European efforts are designed to demonstrate in a practical way our determination to ensure that no time is lost in the search for a solution to a dispute which threatens Western interests and the prospects for world peace.'

Comment: Europe is in no position to ensure anything

about the Middle East and certainly has no influence on a time scale.

Carrington: 'We have made it clear to the Americans that we have no intention of undermining US efforts.'

Comment: This is not how the Americans see the situation. To them undermining has taken place, if only because the 'European initiative' has diverted attention from the main American thrust.

The PLO's achievements in London have been considerable. Farouk Khaddoumi met Sir Ian Gilmour, when he was Deputy Foreign Secretary, at the Syrian Embassy. Sir Ian explained that it was 'nothing more than an unplanned social encounter at a diplomatic reception,' but the PLO attached much greater significance to the event.

In May 1981 Nabil Ramlawi, the PLO's London representative, was appointed Dean of the Arab Diplomatic Corps. The decision, by the Arab ambassadors, was ostensibly because Mr. Ramlawi was the most senior serving head of an Arab mission in London; he was appointed in January 1978. This is the first appointment of a PLO envoy to head the Arab Diplomatic Corps in a non-Arab country, and it was carefully contrived to give impetus to the 'European initiative' at a time when the British Foreign Secretary was to be chairman of the EEC Foreign Ministers Committee.

Chapter Seven

First Convince the Israelis

A PLO propagandist, Professor Fayez Sayegh, once demonstrated for me, in Beirut, his favourite blackboard theorem to rule out proposals that there is room for two nations in the area of Palestine for which the British received the mandate from the old League of Nations after World War I.

'You must understand,' he explained, 'that all this area is one Arab unit, and quite indivisible. We call that Axiom $2 + 2 = 4$. The Jews come with their demand that we recognise their state. That is impossible. We call their demand Axiom $2 + 2 = 6$. When they see that they cannot have their way, they offer us what they term a compromise. They are now willing to make that Axiom $2 + 2 = 5$. It makes no difference. There are eternal truths that are a matter of principle, of yes or no. There can be no answer but 4 to that particular question.'

Sayegh became fond of quoting this theorem, and Israelis, from the relaxed moderate to the tense extremist, produce it as an example of the main obstacle to peace. 'We are not talking about a matter as precise as a mathematical problem,' an Israeli academic told me. 'It's more a mixture of psychology and political science and linguistics. If the PLO says that something we suggest is as absurd as $2 + 2$ equals 6 where can we go from there?'

The view of the Israeli Labour Party, as expressed by its chairman, Shimon Peres, in 1980, is based on figures but is essentially pragmatic.*

* In the Cairo magazine, *October*.

'To solve the problem we have to ask where the Palestinians are. This is only a matter of statistics but it's surprising to see to what extent people ignore them. Nearly half of the Palestinian people live in Jordan and they are a majority of the Jordanian population. Jordan itself in the not-so-distant past was a part of Palestine. About 700,000 other Palestinians live in Judea and Samaria. About 100,000 live in Jerusalem, about 450,000 in the Gaza Strip, about 600,000 are Israeli citizens, and up to 300,000 are refugees in Lebanon.

'We must see the problem and its solution in a unified, complete context. All of the interim solutions must derive from a view of the comprehensive solution at the end of the road. What is the comprehensive solution? Will it be a single solution, or two or three? A single solution means one political framework, one army, one flag. Two solutions means two states, two armies, two flags. We contend that more than one solution is no solution at all, merely a change of venue, date and reason for further conflict. If, for example, a Palestinian state based on the PLO is established, alongside Jordan, Arafat's unceasing attempts to take over Jordan as well—as called for in the Palestinian Covenant—will cause constant terror and tension. King Hussein would respond accordingly. And Israel would find itself involved in this perpetual tension. A Palestinian state with an army equipped for offence would pose a threat to its neighbours on both east and west. But it isn't even clear if such a state would be stable enough to withstand the competition which already exists among the various PLO factions. Katyusha rockets would fly in all directions and the response to them would be continuous escalation of the confrontation in the entire area.

'. . . . For these reasons Israel favours a Jordanian-Palestinian framework which would include all the more than three million Palestinians living today in Jordan, Judea, Samaria and Gaza.'

A perceptive Israeli view of Israel–PLO relations has been expressed by Chaim Herzog, a former Israeli Ambassador to the United Nations. Herzog has long held the view that Israelis should talk with and negotiate with any Palestinian Arabs who recognise Israel's right to exist and who will also decry the use of terror as a weapon.

The provocative point Herzog makes is this: If talks with Palestinians was the official Israeli attitude the weight of US pressure and world opinion would focus on the PLO and call for it to make concessions. But when it is implied by Israeli spokesmen that under no conditions will Israel negotiate then since no price that the PLO might name will apparently make any difference there is no point in putting pressure on the PLO. Thus the pressures concentrate on Israel.

Herzog can also see that sooner or later Israel will face a major crisis—especially in a shift of US policy and public opinion. And while this is happening the PLO is called upon to pay no price at all. He says, 'Had the PLO planned Israeli policy in relation to the PLO it could not have planned it better. Israel's attitude coincides exactly with the political requirements of the PLO—because what Israeli spokesmen are saying is, in effect, that Israel will never negotiate with the PLO under any condition. That is exactly the attitude that the PLO requires from Israel.'

As Herzog sees the game, if the ball was placed firmly in the PLO's court and its National Executive and Council faced the problem of overhauling the Covenant a major internal split would develop. The PLO would be saddled with the major problem of having to tell the world exactly what its purpose is. A bitter internecine dispute would emerge which would clarify to the world the issues facing Israel on the problem.

'Above all,' says Herzog, 'from a political point of view it is essential that a price be set which the PLO would have to pay, a price which would force it out into the open and oblige it to face decisions which it has avoided until now.'

But talking with the PLO is not easy because Israeli thinking is coloured by instinctive distrust of the PLO and the dangers of the creation of a third, PLO-dominated state—the other two being first Jordan and then Lebanon.

Israel's security needs are perpetually underlined by PLO demands and aims.

David Krivine, an Israeli commentator, expresses the problem in these terms:

> If Israel were, say, Spain, it would be easy to give the Basques or Catalonia independence; if Israel were Iran, independence for Kurdistan would not be a problem [because the separatists live in different areas]. But Israel would be asked to create a hostile Arab state in its midst, [in an] area of just 8,000 square miles.*

'Talking to the PLO' has two facets—the personal and the official. Shlomo Hillel, a former Minister of Police and a man who has had many political conversations with Arabs, explains the predicament. It is not a question of whom you talk to but simply what you talk about. 'Of course,' he says, 'I would be civil to a PLO man I happened to meet in a train. There is no law banning civil conversation with anyone—nor any reason for one. But it is a very different matter when people plan political talks with persons who reject our existence. *They* don't go to a meeting to say 'Good morning.' There can be useful talks with representatives of Arab states about borders, about stages of mutual recognition, about matters of common interest. But a private citizen cannot enter into negotiations of even this kind if he disagrees with official policies any more than a soldier can go and shoot at Palestinians in Lebanon if his army does not send him there on a mission.'

Israel is against a Palestinian state but its reasons do not begin and end with security, though this is a major factor. The main objections to Palestinian statehood are perhaps more comprehensive than Israel's enemies comprehend. They are:

* *Jerusalem Post*, September 9, 1979

The economic viability of a totally independent Palestinian state is dubious. It would have no natural resources, an unskilled labour force, practically no industry, limited land for agriculture and a high population density.

The suggested area, already divided into two quite separate parts of the West Bank and the Gaza Strip, would be likely to attract Palestinian immigrants from Lebanon, Jordan and elsewhere. This would further limit its chances of satisfactory economic viability.

A state in economic difficulty from the start would find it hard to establish strong government. This would reduce the chances of effective demilitarisation and increase the possibility of a take-over by militant factions of the PLO.

The PLO would be likely to turn to an outside power for support and its leader, Arafat, already has close links with the Soviet Union. Nothing would please the Russians more than to take over the position of power at the very fulcrum of the Middle East dispute.

The PLO is committed to the destruction of Israel by 'armed conflict'. It has had many chances of modifying this doctrine but is least likely to do so if placed in a position of power.

Israelis believe that not only their own country but the world will run a grave risk if a small, split, unviable, vulnerable and politically inexperienced state is created prematurely in the middle of what has been a particular danger area since 1948, and in a general sense for centuries before that.

The *Guardian*, which rarely sides with the Israeli point of view, agrees with some of this argument.

'The Israelis are right in that close co-operation between Israel and Jordan is necessary for the sensible economic exploitation of the area's natural resources and for overcoming the lack of them. It is not enough for the Palestinians simply to be given a parcel of arid land from which to carve out a miniature republic. The West Bank needs to be one part of a larger economy, providing autonomy for the stateless Palestinian people but sharing in the development which Israel and Jordan can provide. If the laws of politics in that part of the world seem to be temporarily in suspense the dictates of geography cannot be so lightly set aside. The PLO undoubtedly recognises this. It has accepted the notion of a state on any portion of Palestinian land vacated by the Israelis knowing that the state would not be viable. What happens then? The only obvious alternative to a Palestinian state with perpetual designs on its two neighbours is a homeland able to link its economy with both.'*

Israel has proposed the creation of a Palestinian Administrative Council, grouped in 10 divisions, which would deal with virtually every matter affecting the Palestinians. There would be Israeli-Palestinian co-operation in foreign trade, regional planning, water supply and internal security. While the new council was still in the development stage Israel would manage defence and foreign affairs, though these would pass to the Palestinians. The stumbling block to all this is that the Israelis will talk only to "the Palestinians", whom they would protect from PLO terrorists.

The Begin Government's attitude was always that the 'full autonomy' agreed to at Camp David for the West Bank–Gaza region is for the Arab *inhabitants* of those areas, not for the territories themselves. 'What I must make clear, and what must be understood from the outset,' said Israeli Interior Minister Yosef Burg, chairman of the Israeli negotiating team, 'is that autonomy does not and cannot imply sovereignty . . . We must by definition reject *a priori* an independent Palestinian statehood. It

* November 23, 1980

would be a mortal danger to Israel and a grave peril to the whole free world . . . The West Bank is a vital buffer against attacks by Arab armies and Palestinian terrorists.'

Distrust of the PLO is exacerbated by the constant flow of PLO statements received by the Israeli Foreign Ministry in Jerusalem from its embassies. Any single one makes disturbing reading, collectively they are alarming.

Here is a culling of just a few weeks in 1977:

'There are two (initial) phases to our return: the first phase to the 1967 lines, and the second to the 1948 lines . . . the third stage is the democratic state of Palestine. So we are fighting for these three stages.'

Farouk Khaddoumi, in an interview with *Newsweek*, March 1977.

'It is only for political reasons that we carefully stress our Palestinian identity, for it is in the national interest of the Arabs to encourage a separate Palestinian identity to counter Zionism. Yes, the existence of the Palestinian identity serves only tactical purposes. The founding of a Palestinian state is a new tool in the continuing battle against Israel. . . . After we have attained our rights in the whole of Palestine we must not postpone, even for a single moment, the reunification of Jordan and Palestine.'

Zuhair Mohsein, a senior member of the PLO Executive Council, in an interview with the Dutch daily, *Trouw*, March 31, 1977. Mohsein was murdered in a factional intrigue four months later.

'There is no new policy by the PLO to recognise Israel. The declared programme of the PLO is to bring about the destruction of the Zionist entity of Israel.'

PLO Information Office, Oslo, May 5, 1977.

Israel's Gush Emunim ultranationalists have attracted worldwide attention with their zealot demands for unlimited Jewish settlement in the Gaza Strip and West Bank but theirs is far from the prevailing Israeli opinion. The

Peace Now Movement, among whose members are many prominent scholars and politicians, is more representative of public opinion. In April 1980 Professor Yacob Talmon, a leading historian at the Hebrew University of Jerusalem and a staunch Zionist, wrote to the Tel Aviv daily *Ha'aretz*, to denounce the Begin government's idea of Palestinian "autonomy" as an archaic concept. Limited autonomy plans had never worked, he said, and the policy of the Begin government on territory and settlement 'violated the Zionist aim of peace with our neighbours.'

Under certain conditions, Talmon and others would talk with the PLO. For instance, if the PLO, having become the political force within a new state, would accept demilitarisation—apart from weapons needed for internal policing—many Israelis could accept its presence as a neighbour.

While Western Europe professes to see reasonableness in the PLO the Israeli moderates are continually frustrated by lack of any reciprocal sign of moderation from the PLO. In May 1980, Israelis who opposed Jewish settlements on the West Bank and what they considered intimidation of West Bank Arabs, took a full-page advertisement in an Israeli newspaper under the heading 'Their Way is Not Ours.' It was signed by a representative cross-section of Israeli public figures of the Peace Now movement who advocate peaceful dialogue with the Palestinians, not 'the way' of violence.

They hoped for some response from Arab moderates to put their weight against an otherwise inevitable cycle of hatred, incitement and violence. Instead, the Fatah Congress which met a month after the advertisement was published, reaffirmed its policy of liquidating Israel, and called yet again for armed struggle as the only way to achieve its ends.

A well-known Israeli Labour Party politician and editor, Asher Maniv, wrote at the time, 'As an Israeli who has always fought for the cause of moderation and compromise, is it too much to expect some forces of moderation and compromise on the Arab side? Why is it that only the hawks on both sides always give each other the most valuable assistance, each new act of violence and of rejection of compromise 'proving' again that there is nobody to talk to and nothing to talk about? Where is the solidarity of doves on both sides? Or are there none on the Arab side?'*

The frustrated Maniv said, 'There is just so much any Israeli, even the moderate ones, can take. In addition to all his other troubles the Israeli moderate has now to deal with what is called the 'European initiative', which to Israeli eyes can only be seen as the abandonment of Israel by its former friends for the sake of short-term but probably mistaken considerations of petro-self interest.'

At the end of his article Maniv asks: 'If by any chance there are any moderate Palestinians or any reasonable Europeans reading this, do they honestly believe that there are enough people on their sides who can break the vicious circle? I can assure them that there will be no lack of Israeli moderates to help them.'

Maniv's plea might well have been addressed to Western European politicians as much as to the Palestinians, because the 'European initiative' brought into the Israel –PLO dispute two exacerbating factors. In the first place the 'initiative' confused the PLO because it held out hopes which could never be fulfilled. Secondly, it antagonised the Israelis because the Europeans were claiming expert knowledge of the situation when in reality they knew little of its complexities.

Other Israeli moderates include Elkana Galli, a former adviser to Israel's first premier, David Ben-Gurion. 'In the early days, we Jews were in search of our national identity,' he says. 'Now the Palestinians are going through the same search for their national identity. The only foreseeable solution is a territorial compromise.'

Other Israelis agonise over the question of the terms on which they could reach peace with the Palestinians. In March 1981 the Van Leer Institute of Jerusalem held a

*Jerusalem Post, June 15, 1980

symposium which it called 'Is there a solution to the Palestinian problem?'

Various ideas were put forward, most of them beginning from the premise that the Palestinians must have a state. But all foundered on the refusal of the PLO to accept even the most generous Israeli proposal. For instance, the Sheli Party, led by Meir Pa'il, the most left-wing Zionist grouping, requires two states, not one, within the borders of historic Palestine—an Arab state and a Jewish state. The PLO will not accept even this.

Matityahu Steinberg of the Hebrew University, says that his detailed studies indicate that the PLO—in all its factions—has only one aim, to retrieve the whole of Palestine; that is, to eliminate Jewish statehood.

The Israelis become impatient with PLO misquotation and misrepresentation of the two United Nations resolutions 242 and 338, which form the basis for UN policy on the conflict. The Israelis point out that contrary to what PLO propagandists say, there has been no resolution calling for an Israeli withdrawal from all occupied territories. The framers of the resolutions indeed did refrain from using the phrase '*all* the occupied territories,' knowing that it would never have been adopted. The resolutions affirmed the right of every state in the area to live in peace 'within secure and recognised boundaries' and envisaged a negotiated settlement between the parties. The PLO and its supporters, say the Israelis, talk about the resolutions 242 and 338 as though 'withdrawal' is the sole provision of these resolutions. But apart from negotiated settlement, they impose on the parties certain specific obligations, such as an end to belligerency, respect for each other's sovereignty and much else.

Another factor of PLO propaganda which Israelis cannot tolerate is the organisation's continually updated scoresheet of terrorist operations against Israel. The November 1980 issue of *The Palestine Report*, published in London, noted that earlier in the year the Palestinians were carrying out 'resistance operations' at the rate of two every three days. Since the 1967 war over 10,000 commando operations had been carried out against the Israelis.

'The level (of terrorist operations) was maintained in October,' the Report states. 'On October 5 the Abu-Hasan Salameh commando group was responsible for an attack on a post office in the Tel Aviv satellite town of Givatayim, in which three Israelis were killed. . . . In Jerusalem a Molotov cocktail was used in an action near the Damascus Gate . . . while near Jaffa Gate in the early hours another explosion demolished the front of a house.'

'On October 26 three separate commando actions were confirmed. In one incident alone 13 Israeli soldiers were killed or injured when a bomb exploded on the roof of a crowded Army hitch-hiking post on the main road from Jerusalem to Tel Aviv. In the second incident more Israeli troops were injured when another bomb exploded in a bus . . . While earlier a commando threw a hand grenade at an Israeli vehicle.'

Israelis say, 'How is negotiation possible with men who are proud of having carried out 10,000 terrorist operations?' And the PLO responds, 'Negotiate and we will stop our terrorist attacks.' The result is the classic impasse of mutual distrust.

As for European attitudes, the Israelis are alarmed and distressed that in Europe's capitals it is no longer taboo to question Israel's right to exist. A lecturer in history at the Hebrew University of Jerusalem, Moshe Sharon, puts this fact euphemistically: 'Suggestions emanating from Europe about ways of solving the "Palestinian problem" do not exclude the possibility of a total change in the character of the state of Israel.'

The Israelis are particularly fearful of the key West German word in the European solution—"reunification". As they see it, reunification is the "civilised or sophisticated adaptation of the final solution according to the Palestinian Covenant." Sharon says, 'What our "friends" from Europe are kindly advising us, in addition to the establishment of a Palestinian state, is the opening of the gates of pre-1967 Israel to the so-called Palestinian refugees and their descendants. Once this is done, with the Jews becoming almost overnight a minority in Israel proper, the ground will be prepared for reunification. What a civilised word to inscribe on the coffin of the Jewish state.'

Chapter Eight

World Terror

One day in July 1974 while on my way on foot to keep an appointment at a PLO office in Beirut I lost my way and called at a bookshop to ask for directions. At my mention of the PLO establishment the man behind the counter looked up sharply. 'Why do you want that office?' he said.

'Because I have an appointment there.'

'Come into the back room,' he said, taking my arm.

In the back room were seven men, all so tense that they were obvious conspirators. There followed much talk in Arabic—too rapidly spoken for me to follow—and all eyes studied me and my attaché case suspiciously. One man openly took a Beretta automatic from his pocket and put it on a table. I explained that my appointment had been made by a certain lady well connected with George Habash and her name changed the atmosphere; when, very cautiously, I opened my attaché case so that they could see I was unarmed the men relaxed and became friendly. One of them walked with me to my appointment where, as always, a heavily armed guard searched me for weapons.

The small group in the bookshop backroom was a new terrorist cell, one of the scores which have had a brief but hectic life in the violent milieu of southern Lebanon. They spawn with the fertility of mushrooms in the hothouse of terrorism.

All can count on capital finance from Fatah or one of the several major terrorist groups. If they succeed in some exploit against Israel they will be supported even more heavily. In any case, the men concerned will have brought themselves to the notice of the PLO commanders; many have in this way been recruited into the PLO itself as agents to work abroad.

I recount the Beirut story to show, in a small and local way, how terror breeds terror. It has its own momentum. The principle holds good in the world outside the PLO's immediate sphere of operations, as I had seen on another visit to Beirut in 1972 when I interviewed Soraya Antonius, secretary of the Fifth of June Society. Because other foreign visitors were also in the offices the staff went to some trouble to keep us separated but the efforts were inept and I saw three Japanese being taken into Miss Antonius' office. Later I found out that they were members of the Japanese Red Army—the Japanese terrorist organisation. Miss Antonius was not an active terrorist but through her it was possible to reach many PLO leaders, including George Habash.

Through a West German journalist I was present at a meeting in 1977 of young German terrorists in Mannheim and a PLO agent was present as an 'adviser'. While reporting on Basque nationalism in 1978 I met a woman explosives instructor who was posing as Greek; from various statements it was clear that she was really Palestinian. By then PLO involvement in terrorism was practically world wide.

Earlier, from 1965 to 1968, the PLO primarily attacked civilians living in Israel. Its propaganda argument was that terror was the last resort of a desperate, homeless people and hence a legitimate form of political expression. The presentation blurred the distinction between criminal and military action. After 1968 the PLO and its subsidiary bodies exported terror, its targets being Western, Arab, Israeli and Jewish targets within the Middle East and beyond. Between 1968 and 1980 Arab terrorists committed more than 300 different attacks including bombings and shootings, in 26 countries other than Israel; 813 people were killed, 1,013 were injured and more than 90 per cent of the 2,755 hostages were not Israelis. Targets included 40 civil airline planes, five passenger ships and 30 embassies or other diplomatic missions. About 40 economic targets were hit, including fuel depots and factories. More than 30 diplomats were assassinated or wounded and letter bombs were sent to numerous civilians.

From being a small organisation operating solely against Israel the PLO had grown, by the mid-1970s, into the principal co-ordinating, logistic and supply centre for anarchistic and terror groups throughout the world. That it was able to reach this pre-eminent position is the result of several factors, not least being its substantial financial backing, mainly from the Arab oil-producing states. It also gains strength from its extra-territorial status in various Middle Eastern countries—Lebanon, South Yemen, Libya, Iraq, Algeria and Iran under Khomeini, also in Jordan until September 1970 when King Hussein bloodily expelled it from Jordan. Arab governments have granted diplomatic immunity to PLO agents and have applied political pressure on the West on the PLO's behalf. Some governments have provided several diplomatic aids to the PLO, including the supply of false passports, the smuggling of arms through diplomatic bags and the provision of refuge. Libya and Algeria have been most accommodating but for a time Egypt also was helpful.

The South American connection seems to have begun at the beginning of 1971 when a Brazilian revolutionary movement, Vanguarda Popular Revolucionara (VPR), established links with the PLO. The chief PLO agent then in Brazil was Robhi Halloum—arrested the following year in Amsterdam when he was trying to smuggle arms and explosives to Sao Paulo. The VPR has a tactical alliance with PFLP, which sent the first group of Brazilian guerrillas to undergo training in Libya. The present PLO chief in Brazil, Farid Sawan, has a recruitment programme for Brazilians of Arab extraction. Organised in cells, they are obliged to provide money for the PLO network in Brazil while trainees who show real promise are singled out by the PLO's local chief of operations, Taysir Shalabi, for further instruction in the Middle East.

The PLO faction which has worked most actively to establish an international terrorist network is the PFLP, largely financed by Iraq. The late Dr. Wadi Haddad, the PFLP's organiser of international operations, established links with the IRA, the German Baader-Meinhof group, the Japanese Red Army and the Junta de Coordinacion Revolucionara—the umbrella organisation of the South American revolutionaries. He also had close contact with the leaders of Libya, Algeria, Uganda under Idi Amin, and South Yemen. Haddad planned all the PFLP's operations from the first 1968 air hijacking until the kidnapping of the 11 OPEC ministers in 1975. He also planned with Amin's co-operation the hijacking of an Air France plane to Entebbe in June 1976 and the hijacking of a Lufthansa plane to Mogadishu, Somalia, in December 1977. After the overthrow of Amin in 1979 documents were found proving that the PLO had helped to train Amin's murder squads and actively participated in Amin's atrocities.

Haddad's second-in-command was Muhammad Boudia, who attended the Patrice Lumumba University in Moscow where he met the terrorist Carlos, whose real name is Illich Ramirez Sanchez, a Venezuelan. Boudia worked with the Italian terrorist group, the Red Brigades, and helped them to blow up oil tanks in Trieste. He was shot dead in Paris in June 1973, probably by Israeli intelligence.

During 1969 Fatah began to collaborate with neo-Nazi organisations. A Belgian, Jean Tireault, secretary of the neo-Nazi organisation La Nation Europpeenne and co-ordinator of terrorist activity in Brussels, became an adviser to Fatah. Another Belgian neo-Nazi, Karl van der Put, was active in recruiting volunteers for Fatah. The Belgian neo-Nazi bulletin *Alliance* on November 11 that year reported that a secret meeting of former Nazi leaders held in Madrid at the end of August 1969 promised support, including propaganda, instructions and financial support to Fatah. Also that year another former Nazi officer, Johann Schuller, living in Rome, sold arms to Fatah and recruited military instructors.

During 1969 the PFLP, like Fatah, also discovered the

European neo-Nazi groups to be a promising source of aid and encouragement. For example, a former Nazi commander of the German Brandenburg Division during World War II was recruited to command the PFLP training camp at Basra, in southern Iraq.

During the January 1970 trial in Winterthur, Switzerland, of the three captured PFLP terrorists who had attacked an El Al plane in Zurich in February 1969, much data was revealed about the links between Fatah and Swiss neo-Nazis, especially with François Geroude, head of the Swiss Arab Bank and one of the founders of the Swiss Nazi Party. An analysis of the links between the Palestinian Arab terrorist organisations and the radical rightist movements in Europe appeared in an editorial in the Italian daily *Corriere Della Sera* shortly after the bloody Athens attack, on August 5, 1973, on transit passengers from a TWA flight which had originated in Israel. Among other evidence of such ties, the editorial refers to an advertisement which had appeared in the neo-Nazi *Deutsche National und Söldaten Zeitung* for movement members to join the ranks of the PLO terrorists, in order to 'learn the system of war of liberation of the Palestinians.' The editorial also refers to similar links with neo-Nazi groups in Spain, France, Portugal, Argentina and Italy.

On April 6, 1973 the Viennese newspaper *Die Presse* reported that a member of the Austrian neo-Nazi party, Herald Angelke, had been arrested on charges of having introduced into the party a group of Arab terrorists who had been arrested and sentenced to four months' imprisonment. Towards the end of 1975, three German Nazis who had been sought by Interpol for automobile and document theft—Guenther Brahburg, Eckhardt Will and Gunnar Fahl—were caught in Yugoslavia. At their trial, on January 26, 1976, their Nazi lawyer, Wilhelm Staller, revealed that the three had been to a PLO training camp in the Middle East. Intelligence sources also reported at the time that there had been contacts between the Black September wing of Fatah and the radical rightist Arab-German Liberation Front, based in West Germany.

An agreement was reached in 1977 between the radical rightist L'oeuvre Française and Fatah, according to which the PLO terrorist organisation would train members of the French group and it, in return, would conduct terrorist operations on behalf of Fatah, when called upon to do so.

On January 8, 1978 the Yediot Aharonot correspondent in Bonn reported that four members of the Free Corps-Adolph Hitler and Free Corps-Saudi Arabia radical right-wing groups had been arrested in West Germany on suspicion of having had contacts with members of the PLO in West Germany and of having smuggled arms from Arab states to that country. They had been caught red-handed while smuggling arms, and at least one of them was in possession of a membership card in the PLO.

An Associated Press report from Zurich quoted a spokesman of the Bavarian Interior Ministry as having said on October 1, 1980 that there 'appeared to be links' between the illegal neo-Nazi Wehrsportgruppe Hoffman gang—which was responsible for the bomb attack, in late September of 1980, on Munich's Oktoberfest, in which 12 persons were killed and 213 injured—and the PLO.

Since about 1976 the PLO has played a key role as a co-ordinating body for revolutionary groups of both the far right and the left outside the Middle East. The *Irish Times* reported in June 1978 that the PLO was training IRA terrorists in southern Lebanon and that UN officers in the area were aware of this. A NATO report showed that in 1979 1,912 non-Arab recruits had military training and ideological indoctrination courses at nine Palestinian camps—Hamouriyah near Damascus and the 'September 17' base in Syria; Burj al-Barajna, Shatilla, Katirmaya and Damour in Lebanon; Ras Hilal in Libya; Sani-San near Baghdad in Iraq and Socotra in South Yemen.

The largest single contingent, 580, came from Iran; 306 Turks attended PLO courses, mostly in Syria but also in the Beirut suburbs and in Libya. In that year, too, an estimated 44 members of the IRA received training at Palestinian camps, including 15 at Damour, 10 in Socotra and seven in Burj al-Barajna. According to an Irish deserter who became an informer for the American FBI, contact between the PLO and the IRA is routine, the liaison officer being a young Arab woman living in Dublin. At higher level PLO and IRA seniors meet either in Cyprus or Athens.

The Italian Red Brigades sent 32 men and women for training, and Japan's Red Star Army, 21. Spanish terrorists numbered 113, many of them ETA members. Spaniards receive their training at 'September 17' camp and at Hamouriyah.

In November 1980 Western intelligence sources had evidence that more than 2,000 terrorists from outside the Middle East, including Polisario guerrillas from the Western Sahara, were receiving training at PLO camps in Arab countries. According to *The Daily Telegraph*, on June 6, 1980, Hamouriyah camp counted among its trainees four West Germans; six Italian members of the Red Army and Red Brigades terrorist networks; four Red Army members from Japan; three members of the Spanish Basque terrorist organisation, ETA; 28 Argentinian members of the Montoneros group; 12 Brazilians, mostly members of the VPR; 130 Armenian Turks, opponents of the conservative government of Suleyman Demirel in Ankara; 130 recruits from various African countries; 32 Asians, many of them from the Philippines; and 170 Iranians, who attended courses under an agreement between Abbas Zamani, chief of Ayatollah Khomeini's Revolutionary Guards, and the head of the PLO office in Teheran, Hanni al-Hassen, a highly influential adviser to the Iranian regime. Zamani had been trained at a Fatah base in Lebanon.

While PLO instructors make up most of the staff of the training centres East Germans and Cubans appear to have considerable authority, with the power to suggest further training for selected recruits in the Soviet bloc countries.

During 1980-81 the number of foreigners attending PLO training courses increased steadily, reflecting the key role of the organisation and its natural security in sympathetic countries. The PLO provides sanctuary for European terrorists at PLO camps after they carry out their acts

103

of sabotage, kidnapping and murder in Europe—as was the case after the murder of the German industrialist Hans Martin Schleyer and of the Premier of Italy, Aldo Moro.

PLO groups have taken part in joint operations with overseas terrorist groups. In January 1974 a band of Arab and Japanese terrorists attacked oil depots in Singapore and in December 1976 the international terrorist Carlos, two Palestinians and three West Germans collaborated to seize the OPEC oil ministers hostage in Vienna. In June 1976 West German and Palestinian terrorists co-operated in the hijacking of an Air France plane to Entebbe, Uganda.

The PLO and overseas terrorist groups routinely supply each other with arms, false documents, money and bases for local operations. They also carry out missions on behalf of each other. The 1972 Lod airport massacre, for example, was perpetrated by the Japanese Red Army for the PLO while, in 1977, the latter hijacked a Lufthansa airliner for the Baader-Meinhof gang.

The PLO and the Khomeini regime in Iran share an idealogical commitment to the use of terror as a political weapon, and have in common a hatred of the West. Long before the overthrow of the Shah, the PLO supported the Iranian underground with money, arms and training. One of Ayatollah Khomeini's first acts in power was publicly to thank the PLO for its part in the Iranian revolution. The strength of the connection between Khomeini and Arafat was shown late in 1979 when 10 million dollars was transferred from the Central Bank in Teheran to the PLO in Beirut; this operation was supervised by the son of the important Ayatollah Montazhari.

The PLO and its subsidiaries are involved with yet other groups. Dutch 'Red Aid' members have been trained in a PFLP camp in South Yemen and took part in an abortive attempt to hijack an Air France flight to Tel Aviv Airport in September 1976. Norwegian, Swiss and Belgian nationals are known to have been involved with PLO activities.

In September 1980 the PLO spread its direct activities

to Central America when its agents planned to kidnap the French ambassador to Costa Rica, in order to exchange him for four Palestinian terrorists seized in France after an abortive attempt to assassinate Shahpur Bakhtiar, the former Prime Minister of Iran and an enemy of the Ayatollah Khomeini. The four Palestinians include one highly regarded by the PLO leaders—Walid Husni el-Hadj. He had attacked the Iraqi embassy in Paris in July 1978, and in a bloody shoot-out a French police inspector was killed. During the attempt on Bakhtiar's life another policeman was killed as well as a woman who lived on the same landing as Bakhtiar.

The plot came to light on September 11 when the US ambassador in Costa Rica told his French counterpart, Michel Dondenne, that American intelligence suspected a terrorist attempt to kidnap him. Dondenne had already been the victim of a political kidnapping in May 1979, while serving in El Salvador. He was released after payment of a ransom. According to the Americans, Dondenne would be kidnapped while travelling on the road to the stadium for the commemoration of Costa Rica's national day or during a reception at the Foreign Ministry.

Uneasiness spread throughout the diplomatic corps and finally only the American and Spanish ambassadors attended the celebrations, unaccompanied by their wives. Later the Brazilian ambassador revealed the plot; PLO agents had been for months in contact with revolutionary movements in Latin America which had agreed to provide cover for the PLO snatch.

Claire Sterling, author of *The Terror Network*, the most authoritative book on international terrorist conspiracy, says that without the 'pretext' of the Palestinian movement, world terrorism would never have reached its present proportions. At a press conference this question was put to Miss Sterling: 'Now that we are aware of the aid given to the Palestinians one has a better understanding of the interest of the Soviets in promoting terrorism. It is said that the Palestinians have succeeded in infiltrating hundreds of agents into the United States and that they are only waiting for the five years necessary to obtain American nationality. Do you believe in the real possibility of an outburst of terrorism in the United States?'

Her answer was: 'Undoubtedly. It's surprising that this hasn't happened already. Terrorism has reached such a point of organisation that anyone who wishes to join can become a terrorist.'

According to Miss Sterling, the PLO has all the qualifications necessary to attract a neo-Fascist organisation which itself advocates anti-Semitism. The PLO has thus gained the support of the international 'black order'—that is, terrorism not necessarily involved with Leftish revolutionaries.

PLO involvement in terrorism can be found right from the beginning, says Miss Sterling, and refers to two Algerians from Fatah at a convention in Barcelona in 1969. The occasion was a conference called by the Lausanne-based neo-Nazi Europaeische Neue Ordnung. The Algerians attempted to focus the convention's attention on the Palestinian issue and to recruit members to Fatah. Miss Sterling says, 'They easily obtained political, financial and above all technical support for widespread terrorist training. At that time Fascists were organising and directing training camps all over Europe and especially in Spain. The Palestinians were very welcome there.'

Wherever else in the world the PLO terrorists might have been welcome, by 1981 their freedom to move against Israel was being greatly curtailed. Israeli forces were making strikes by land, sea and air against the PLO's military bases in southern Lebanon, either to pre-empt an attack or to retaliate for the firing of rockets against Israeli settlements. US National Security adviser Richard Allen said that there was 'ample justification for taking actions to reach the source of terrorism.' With the Israel–Lebanon border and the Mediterranean coast tightly secured, the PLO resorted to tactics bordering on the bizarre.

In March the PLO sent two apparently badly trained and demonstrably unsure gunmen at night across the border with Lebanon in fragile hang-gliders. The strange episode unintentionally demonstrated the military weakness of the terrorist factions. The air crossing with all its risks was undertaken only because infiltration by land and sea had become too difficult.

In July 1980 terrorists tried to cross the border in a hot-air balloon. The balloon caught fire and crashed in south Lebanon, killing the four men aboard.

International terrorism, especially with Russian involvement, is not likely to degenerate into such ineffectual games.

In Paris in March 1982 PLO gunmen murdered Ya'acov Bar-Simantov, a counsellor at Israel's Paris Embassy and June 3, 1982 a hit team shot the Israeli Ambassador to Britain, Shlomo Argov. These shootings were planned as the first steps in a new wave of terrorism directed at Israeli diplomats and foreign supporters of Israel. They were among the causes of the Israeli attacks against the PLO in Lebanon ten days later.

Chapter Nine

Schools for Terror

Terrorism as a form of political expression has no meaning unless it is supported by physical and moral terrorism. Throughout the century until the mid-1960s terrorist inciters believed that they had only to give a man a bomb or a revolver and encourage him to throw it or fire it at "the enemy." These agents provocateur gave their agents no training in how or where to use their weapons and it was not even considered essential that they should know how they worked.

Fatah was the world's first organisation to embark upon systematic training for terrorism and the other groups within the PLO soon followed. From the military point of view such training made good sense; for terrorism to thrive it must be seen to be successful—and greater success could only come from efficient training.

The first properly structured terrorist schools, with instructors and facilities, were set up in the refugee camps of southern Lebanon. Since 1966 they have proliferated, spreading to Syria, Iraq, Yemen, Egypt, Libya, Algeria, Kuwait, Uganda, the Soviet Union, East Germany, Czechoslovakia, Bulgaria and Yugoslavia. At their most efficient they encompass most of the activities of a British jungle warfare training school, a guerrilla warfare centre and a commando training unit. Having been involved in all three first as a trainee and later as an instructor, I have noted many similarities in the training of PLO terrorists.

The instructors are not always themselves terrorists.

Many come from regular army units and are specialists in the use of explosives and booby traps, small-arms, camouflage, field survival, attacks against underwater targets, and in assassination. Seconded from the armies of Libya, Algeria or Syria, these men do a tour of duty in some terrorist camp and then return home. Other teachers are Palestinians who have been specially trained as instructors in Arab countries, in the Soviet and Eastern-bloc countries. Their training has been extensive and expensive and they are rarely permitted to take part in terrorist attacks. Yet another group of instructors are secretive men from special Russian and East German units who visit terrorist camps to impart particular knowledge—about the recognition and killing of enemy intelligence agents, for instance.

In the PLO's early days a would-be terrorist only needed to show enthusiasm; he would be given some basic training in the use of a Katyusha rocket launcher and sent off to pick his own target and do what damage he could. In some cases small groups of raiders were armed with machine-guns and simply told 'Go and kill Israelis.'

Because they often made the mistake of attacking Israeli army units the terrorists' losses were high; they suffered, too, when they openly attacked a kibbutz in the pattern of the Arab attacks on Jewish settlements in the 1920s and 1930s; the Jewish defenders were usually better trained and could retaliate quickly.

The PLO has long made use of women and girls as terrorists, but in the beginning they too were given cursory instruction. Fatmah Burnawi, a nurse in the West Bank town of Kalkilya, was an underground member of Fatah as early as 1965. The Israelis arrested her for the attempted demolition of the Zion Cinema, Jerusalem, in 1968. Miriam Shakhashir, of Nablus, was 19 when she planted bombs in the Hebrew University cafeteria; the Odeh sisters—Rasmia, 23, Laila, 21 and Achia, 18, put bombs in a supermarket in Jerusalem. A group of schoolgirls from Ramallah sent poisoned chocolates to various enemies, including their own headmaster, an Arab.

During the period 1964 to 1970 the guerrilla theories of Guevara, Mao, Fanon and Giap whom the terrorist spokesmen held up as their mentors, were learned by heart but poorly applied on the ground. Terrorists, though ambitious, lacked stability and resourcefulness and showed all the defects which stem from inadequate training.

Despite changing times the PLO leadership recognised that there would always be a need for the bomb-throwing enthusiast who needed no particular training. Such a man, or boy, could carry out an attack which would strike at the whole fabric of Israeli society. For instance, on January 21, 1971, the Arroyo family, recent Jewish immigrants from Britain, took a short cut while driving home from a visit to the Negev desert. A schoolboy of 15 waved down the car as if asking for a lift—then he lobbed a grenade into the back seat. It killed two children, Mark, 7, and Abigail, 4, and smashed their mother's spine. The PFLP had paid the boy the equivalent of £6 for the attack, which did indeed distress the whole state of Israel.

But such attacks could be counter-productive because they were not selective enough and by mid-1972 the PLO groups had killed nearly 300 of their own people and wounded 1,385, including many women and children; in the same period they killed 50 Israelis and wounded 350. The futility of haphazard attacks was driven home to the PLO on February 1, 1971 when a terrorist set off a bomb in a Gaza post office—and injured 61 Arabs. Israelis never used this post office.

It had already become apparent that enthusiasm was not enough and from 1970 training became more systematic. The Ashbal—"Lion Cubs"—organisation had been set up for junior terrorists, boys from the age of six. 'We are not just a paramilitary organisation,' an Ashbal leader told me in 1972. 'This is a morale-building and educational movement to prepare the well-rounded citizen of Palestine —equipped and trained to defend his nation but also to be a good, productive citizen.' When I saw these boys they were being taught to chant, 'Oh Zionists, do you think you are safe? Drinking blood is the habit of our men.' When ordered to stand at ease, they shout 'Asifa!' (Storm) When

111

they stamp to attention they bellow 'Fatah!' At the end of training sessions the boys stand to attention and chant their Fatah credo: 'I have shattered the manacles limiting my freedom and I have arisen like a hurricane to break out of my prison and free my country.'

Their first task when building a camp is to dig a slit trench for mock battle in which they play at storming an Israeli outpost. Each raid reaches its climax as the attacking group storms the enemy position, shouting, 'We are from Fatah! We have come to kill you all!'

Youths and young men destined to carry out planned terrorist attacks in Israel or in other countries were carefully selected. They had to be intelligent enough to learn not only how to fire a weapon but how to repair and service it, not only how to use explosive but how to make it from materials openly bought in shops. Many terrorists had been caught by Israeli troops because they had taken up positions from which there was no retreat; now they were given better military training. Hours of instruction also went into "selection of targets." It was pointless, trainees were told, to fire a rocket at a lone Israeli farmer on a tractor, when better targets were available.

On January 15, 1971, terrorists killed a Druze tractor driver, Hussein Sharif Abu Hamad, while he was working in a field on the slopes of Mount Hermon; they decapitated him and took his head back to Lebanon. A year later an engineer, Josef Gruber, 24, of Haifa was alone in a jeep on an early morning inspection tour of construction work near Golan Heights when he was shot at close range. His attackers decapitated him and defiled his body.

Both attacks were probably carried out by freelance terrorist groups. The PLO leadership approved because the death of any Israeli was to be applauded but training officers were again told to discourage assaults which yielded so little. Better training in reconnaissance would produce a better selection of targets. The PFLP exploit of May 1970 is often used by instructors as an example of "productivity"—to use George Habash's term. A group of his men crossed 500 yards into Israel and prepared an ambush with a bazooka firing 82-mm shells. They had been trained to ignore military targets—and on this occasion they allowed an army patrol in a truck to pass.

They were waiting for a bright yellow bus on its usual morning run from Avivim Moshav, carrying five- to eight-year-olds to school. When the bus slowed for a turn in the road the PFLP men fired three rounds at a range of 20 yards. The driver, two teachers and seven children were killed instantly, another pupil and teacher died later and the other 20 children were wounded.

Since then raids have been even more "productive." On March 10, 1978 a PLO gang from Lebanon reached the Israel coast by dinghy. They learned precisely where they were—near Haifa—by talking to an unsuspecting American woman tourist. After killing her the terrorists hijacked two public buses. Loading their hostages onto one bus the terrorists drove 30 miles along the highway towards Tel Aviv, firing on passing cars. Before they were stopped by a police road block they had killed 36 men, women and children and wounded 76.

I have already mentioned that at least one terrorist school had full-size dummy aircraft for practising the art of hijacking. Detailed plans of every type of passenger aircraft are available from the PLO's central intelligence department, and the movements of cabin staff have been studied and reported. As a matter of routine, agents make more or less regular flights, to observe any change in aircraft security procedure. Much information can be obtained from the International Air Transport Association of which the PLO is an observer member. The PFLP has always made a point of studying airports. In 1970 they considered Athens and Rome to be the most vulnerable and in the 1980s they still held this ranking; security had not appreciably improved despite terrorist attacks.

The efficacy of specialist training became apparent in 1972 with several successful acts of sabotage—on the Trieste oil refineries, August 5, the aircraft engine plant in Hamburg, February 2, and the Ravenstein oil refineries, Holland, February 6. In that year, too, Black September organised, on May 8, the difficult operation of hijacking a Sabena airliner to Tel Aviv airport, though an Israeli subterfuge thwarted their aim of having 100 terrorists released from Israeli prisons. On May 30 a second Tel Aviv airport operation took place when Japanese terrorists, acting for the PFLP, killed 26 people and wounded 80 others. And in September occurred the vicious Munich massacre, when 11 Israeli athletes attending the Olympic Games were killed. The PLO carried out several other coups that year, which the PLO regards as the commencement of "real" terrorism—that is, the training programmes were now paying dividends.

One PLO training department deals solely with terror itself; that is, the psychology of terror rather than its tactics, which are taught separately. Here again the PLO groups were first in the field. Before it introduced methods of heightening terror this had been merely the natural result of a hijack or an embassy take-over or a raid. The PLO brought into its schools psychologists with specialised knowledge of "the fear factor". The most efficient of these instructors were Russian and Bulgarian though after 1978 Syrians, Iraqis and Palestinians themselves largely took over from the Russians.

Trainees are taught that the greatest terror can be inflicted on adults by threats, either explicit or implicit, against children. Such threats have been made many times against those Israeli Arabs who have not been ready enough to help the PLO with safe houses, money and information. Pupils of terrorism are also told that uncertainty engenders fear and that hostages should never be given information of any kind. Discomfort should be inflicted wherever possible; for instance, hostages should not be allowed to go to the lavatory or even to stand up. "A standing man begins to regain confidence," trainees are told. "Should any one male hostage appear to be a dominant personality he should be killed." The captain of the Lufthansa plane hijacked to Mogadishu in October 1977 was killed for this reason.

As for women hostages, terrorist teaching is to refuse to

allow them to comb their hair or to use make-up; this is calculated to break their morale. The practice comes straight from the KGB manual on treatment of political prisoners. 'Terror must be seen to be terrifying,' students are told. 'Making people half afraid means nothing. They must really believe that their lives are in danger. Then they never forget.'

Terrorists posted to Western capitals are taught how to be menacing over the telephone or in anonymous letters. Such tactics are used against Europeans, Americans and South Americans who are classified as anti-PLO or pro-Israeli.

For a select group of educated and intelligent trainees there is a course in "intellectual infiltration." These men and women are not expected to use explosives or firearms and are not terrorists in the accepted sense, but they are an integral part of the terrorist organisation. Usually recruited from among Palestinians educated in foreign countries they are returned to those countries as overt or covert PLO agents. The best of them become "envoys-in-expectation," that is, they are in place for the day when the PLO has a state. Others are assigned to work on sympathisers within a particular country, either to campaign for Palestinian statehood or to agitate against Israel. Their principal targets are politicians, whether in parliament or not, but they are also taught how to approach other influential people. A notebook kept by a student at a course in Tripoli, Libya, contains this statement: 'In England we should appeal to Englishmen on the "underdog theory." The English will help anybody they consider to be oppressed. At the same time we should stress anything which could be considered romantic. The English are impressionable and respond to ideas of chivalry and to ethnic culture. When you invite an Englishman to dinner give him an Arab meal, if possible in an Arab setting. Treat him respectfully but not slavishly (sic)." I take this to mean that the agent should not be obsequious. Students are cautioned against offering an Englishman money as he resents bribes; instead they should offer to "pay expenses" or "contribute to trusts and research," or "make donations to pro-Arab causes."

These intellectual commandos are taught that the most effective approach to the French is through self-interest. 'If the Frenchman can see some monetary or political gain in whatever you suggest he is already supporting you,' the notes say. After the European statesmen adopted their idea of a European initiative some PLO agents were recalled to the Middle East for refresher courses in how to create diplomatic opportunities.

Male and female terrorists are taught how to approach members of the opposite sex in target countries, with the intention of winning their sympathy. PLO women agents are directed to make contact, as a priority, with foreign journalists while their male counterparts are taught the advantages of having a foreign national as a girlfriend. Inexperienced girls can easily be induced to take packages on board aircraft without asking about their contents, as did two 18-year-old British girls on holiday in Rome in August 1972. Two terrorists picked them up and treated them to 11 days of luxury living before suggesting that they all go to Israel; they bought four tickets on an El Al flight. The men then said that for business reasons they could not make the flight on the day planned but urged the girls to go ahead; they would all meet later in Tel Aviv. As "a present and pledge of friendship" they insisted that the girls take a cassette player—which had been fitted with a bomb. El Al men refused to allow the player into the cabin and placed it in the plane's reinforced hold; the time-bomb explosion was not serious enough to damage the plane, which landed safely. Other European girls, mainly Dutch and German, have been seduced into spying for the PLO, into smuggling arms and explosives and even into taking part in rocket attacks on aircraft. Inducing them to do so is part of the PLO's training programme.

A full course in terrorism for men and women being trained for long-term activity in foreign countries can last up to a year, with instruction at several specialist schools. Apart from the standard lessons in explosives, firearms and the techniques of physical and moral violence, subjects include photography, forgery, languages, cryptography, oratory and disguise.

Terrorists chosen for a raid against Israel, in which they have little chance of surviving death or capture, are not of high intellectual calibre. Their training has been largely military with a heavy emphasis on indoctrination, based on the duty they owe to Islam. Many leave on their mission expecting to become "martyrs" and therefore to reach paradise immediately after death at the hands of Israeli soldiers. Their main aim is to kill as many Israelis as possible. To this end their training has been designed to make them persist in the face of all the odds against them and not to surrender. Certain terrorist coups, such as the raids and massacres of children at the kibbutzim of Kiriyat Shemona and Maalot, show that the training has been horrifyingly successful.

How to acquire and use money is another important part of a terrorist's training. The average terrorist needs about 50,000 dollars a year to sustain life in the underground; he must have weapons, several residences, and forged documents, for example. In the case of PLO terrorists money is not a problem but foreign sources can dry up for other nationals, such as the Spanish and German terrorists, and they must then rely on bank robberies. Training in this activity is given by European instructors, apparently East Germans, in the PLO's Middle East centres, which cannot be penetrated by Interpol agents.

South Yemen has become a major training centre, mainly because its geographically isolated position gives it a high degree of invulnerability from attack and security from spies. At any moment in South Yemen, in the three camps at Hauf, Mukalla and Al-Gheidha, about 700 Cubans, backed up by 1,500 Russians and 116 East Germans, are training terrorists from all over the world. Trainees have included members of the German Red Army Faction and the South Moluccans of the Netherlands. In May 1980 a new Dutch terrorist group, Rood

Verzetsfront (Red Resistance Front) returned home after intensive training. The Egyptian Magazine, *October*, reported on May 16, 1978: 'South Yemen has turned the island of Socotra into a stronghold for the Palestinian terror organisations and for terrorists from many countries. Soviet experts are also operating on the island.'

Yet the Soviet attitude to the PLO was at first cool and, before 1968, the more militant Palestinians were even sometimes denounced in the Soviet press as reactionary and ultra-revolutionary. But China had recognised the PLO in 1964 and while the Chinese could not do much for the Palestinians the Russians could see that unless *they* were more helpful the Palestinians and Arabs generally might develop a pro-Chinese orientation. So the Russians became more friendly and liberally supplied weapons. When they offered training to Fatah, to the PFLP and PDFLP, the PLO–Moscow union was firmly set.

By 1978 hundreds of Palestinians were being given advanced terrorist training in 40 top-security schools, mostly in the Moscow suburbs, also at Baku, Tashkent and Odessa. The Bulgarian school is at Varna, in East Germany at Finsterwalde and in Czechoslovakia at Karlovy Vary and Doupov. A course is attended by up to 60 PLO trainees, drawn from the various groups according to a quota system.

The routine is well established. Carrying doctored Jordanian, Iranian or Lebanese passports, the recruits travel to Moscow, where they are met by Al-Amid Al-Sha'ar and Hikmat Abu Zaid, respectively the director and deputy director of the PLO office.

The first lectures are about the achievements of the Bolshevik revolution and the advantages of the Soviet order. After aptitude tests those Palestinians considered above average are transferred for special courses to KGB schools—though they are not allowed to meet the intelligence officers from Libya, Syria, Iraq and South Yemen who are trained there.

According to Herbert Krosney, who produced a television programme on the PLO for the Canadian Broadcasting Corporation, between 1974 and September 1979 at least 1,000 Palestinians had been trained in the Soviet Union or Eastern-bloc countries.

Krosney describes a training camp at Sanprobal near Simferapol on the Black Sea:

There, for six months, the Palestinians—along with activists from Libya, Iraq, South Yemen and Algeria—are given an arduous course of study, including basic military field exercises, communications techniques and lectures in theory. But at the heart of all this instruction comes extensive "engineering" classes. . . .

The syllabus includes the following:
Study of regular and electronic detonators
Training in chemical and biological warfare
Production of incendiary devices
Preparation of an electrical charge by means of a detonator
Study of exploding metals
Crossing rivers by rubber or wooden boats
Study of fuse types—detonating cord-red; instantaneous fuse-red; safety fuse-black.
Blowing up of vehicles, ammunition dumps, petrol tanks
Preparation of anti-personnel minefields.

The Russian connection is well established and its strength was confirmed by Zehdi Labib Terezi, the PLO's representative at the United Nations, in an interview with the American television network, PSB, September 25, 1979.

Question: Mr. Terezi, in the film we have just seen, a number of Palestinians describe the support and the training they've received in the Soviet Union. Can you quantify Soviet support? Can you tell me what kind of support the Soviet Union gives to your organisation?

Terezi: Well, the Soviet Union, and all the socialist countries, they give us full support—diplomatic, moral, educational, and also open their military academies to some of our freedom fighters.

Question: Can you guess how many of your people have gone through military training in the Soviet Union?

Terezi: I don't really know the numbers, but I do know that the availability is there . . .

Question: And the military equipment, is that support given directly to the PLO?

Terezi: Oh, yes. Oh, yes. We're getting those machine guns and RJV's and . . . explosives.

Question: Some American analysts suggest that much of the equipment is funnelled through the existing states of the region.

Terezi: We get our direct consignments that come to the PLO.

Question: To go back to the film. Hader, the defector [in the film] and others talk quite freely about the support they receive from the Soviet Union.

Terezi: There is no secret about that. I mean our boys go to the Soviet Union. They go to the socialist countries. They go everywhere for their training, for their education. There's no secret about that . . . this is something done in the open.

Question: The defector talks about Soviet orders being given to the PLO. He says that Yasser Arafat meets with the Soviet Ambassador in the Lebanon once a week and that the Palestinian organisation now takes orders from the Soviet Union. What do you say to that?

Terezi: . . . He meets with him once a week—I think sometimes he should meet with him twice a day . . .

On another occasion Terezi, while acknowledging the Soviet connection defended it by noting that 'PLO freedom fighters do not have the luxury of choosing their supporters.' He also defended certain terrorist incidents —while regretting injury to innocent women and children —by explaining that the means are not as important as the ends, in this case the "liberation" of the Palestinian homeland.

Soviet leaders have grown to consider the PLO a particularly useful organisation. It can supply subversive agents to be put to work in the Gulf sheikhdoms and in Saudi Arabia; PLO men and women can do jobs all over the world without implicating the Soviet Union, and they make excellent high-level bodyguards, such as those who worked for Idi Amin in Uganda. No other terrorists, from whatever nation, have as many potential functions as the Palestinians, the Russians believe.

The PLO as an organisation has yet another use for the Soviet; it can serve as middleman in supplying arms to the 'national liberation movements,' to which the Soviet is committed under Article 28 of its 1977 constitution. The PLO itself has many Soviet-made arms, including several types of anti-tank and anti-aircraft missiles, artillery, as well as the Czech-made Skorpion sub-machine-gun. The PFLP has used Soviet-made heat-seeking Strela missiles in a series of unsuccessful attacks on civilian airliners.

Professor Charles Horner of Georgetown University, Washington DC, explains that the PLO does not discredit itself by acknowledging that there is such a thing as state-supported terrorism.

Rather, it confirms that it is possible to create a state out of terrorism—a new stage, one suspects, in the theory and practice of revolution. All this has the further advantage of giving to groups like the PLO a form of international respectability. Far from demeaning the PLO in the eyes of the Western democracies, they elevate it. The Soviets understand that this is true, and they see their own influence grow thereby. They become our guide in these matters; those whom they 'recognise' politically first, we will recognise diplomatically in our turn—sooner or later. Put more concretely, it is at precisely the point when the Western democracies can no longer deny the facts of the relationship between the PLO and the Soviet Union that they begin to afford the organisation greater respectability.*

Whether the PLO and its groups have carried out direct assignments for the Soviet Union cannot be proved but some observers, notably Professor Horner and the British journalist Robert Moss, suggest that there is evidence to support the suspicion. One such case was the complex PLO plot to blow up fuel depots in West Berlin and another was the attempt by a Palestinian hit-team in Holland in 1975 to hijack a train carrying Jewish refugees from the Soviet Union.

By 1977 the Russian training had become so effective that, in some techniques, the PLO was training Russians in its Middle East schools. The schooling mainly concerns Arab politics, the Islamic religion and Middle East life-styles. Contingency 'hit plans' are in existence for most Middle East leaders. Other terrorists from Latin and Central America, from Japan, Africa and Europe are constantly passing through PLO training centres, but the PLO will send its instructors abroad, on request. During 1978 two Palestinian experts on booby traps visited Ireland to advise the IRA on the use of bombs in vehicles.** PLO men have become proficient in this tactic, having carried out—by their own estimate—about 1200 such attacks.

Thomas McMahon, found guilty in Dublin of Lord

* *Commentary Magazine*, June 1980
** *Daily Telegraph*, London, 29.9.1978

Mountbatten's murder in 1979, was taught how to make bombs and set them off by remote control during a training period in a PLO camp in Libya, though his supervisors were probably Russian. The terrorist training centre is at Sebhah, 180 kilometres south of Tripoli.

According to the Institute for the Study of Conflict, London, Libya arranged for the delivery of Soviet-made arms to the IRA, the Baader-Meinhof network in Western Germany, the Japanese Red Army, the Arm of the Arab Revolution (Carlos' group) and to insurgents in Turkey, Yemen, Chile and the Philippines. PLO members carried out or supervised many of the deliveries.

Baader-Meinhof members were trained in Lebanon in bacteriological and chemical warfare, apparently because they intended at the time—during 1979—to contaminate water supplies and large-scale ventilation systems. The PLO has stocks of bacteriological and chemical weapons but has not used them against Israel for fear of reprisals of the same kind. During 1980 and 1981 the PLO schools trained German neo-Nazis in Lebanon with emphasis —by request—on assassination and demolition.

PFLP instructors trained the members of the Basque organisation Banta, which kidnapped Spain's ambassador to Lebanon in September 1980, while the PDFLP has a contract to train Corsican separatists. During 1981 the PLO's London office developed links with the British New Communist Party.

At times the PLO has arranged "special" courses for particular groups. At the request of extreme left-wing groups in Turkey in 1978 they set up a training pro-gramme suitable for the prevailing political and military situation. One aspect of training concerned how to attack police stations, often by planting a bomb during an apparently innocent call at the station. The Turks were also taught how one man could distract the attention of a policeman while a second man sniped him from a distance. The Israeli consul in Ankara was assassinated by Turks trained by the PLO. The Turkish General Ergun Gok-deniz reported in an Army magazine that the PLO has armed Turkish rebels and he alleges that the Russians have trained the PLO "in wars of liberation to be fought on Marxist-Lenist methods," which the PLO instructors then passed on to the Turks.

Despite its strong ties with the Soviet Union the PLO has not cut its connections with China. In 1970 Arafat made his first public and official trip to Peking and late that year China took an increasing part in training PDFLP recruits. It considered the PDFLP more "amenable" than Habash's PFLP which the Chinese criticised as irresponsible after the 1970 hijackings.

The PLO has neglected no aspect of training. Its major terrorist amphibious training centre is at Benghazi, Libya, which is far enough from Israel to deter the Israelis from striking at it. Because of Israeli raids, training at the PLO amphibious warfare school at Tyre, southern Lebanon, has been curtailed.

Terrorism at sea has been relatively little practised, though during 1971 the PFLP claimed credit for the attack on the tanker *Coral Sea*, 78,000 tons, near the Straits of Bab el Mandeb. A speedboat fired 10 bazooka-type shells, causing some damage to the tanker. The attack was intended to deter oil exporters from using the Israeli Red Sea port at Eilat. In June 1978 seven specially trained PLO terrorists loaded a 600-ton freighter in Lebanon with 42 Katyusha rockets and three tons of explosives to attack the Eilat oil terminal; an Israeli warship stopped the freighter about 60 miles from the target and sank it. The PLO accepts that major seaborne attacks of this kind are beyond its present capability. The emphasis is on assault-boat raids on Israeli coastal resorts, at least two of which have been spectacularly successful in terms of casualties inflicted, that on the Savoy Hotel, Tel Aviv, in March 1975 and the Haifa Highway massacre.

Training is so diverse and is taken so seriously that the PLO in 1978 created an affiliate organisation, the Palestinian Administrative Development Institute (PADI) to run management training courses in Beirut. Graduation ceremonies are held and a high-ranking PLO official always attends; frequently it is Abu al-Walid. These courses are not directly terroristic but terrorists are among the students. PADI is partly designed to give the PLO a respectable face in the management-minded West and is an integral part of a master plan which can only be seen as extraordinarily sophisticated.

The newest PLO training, with international connections, is for attacks on offshore oil rigs and nuclear power plants; both are considered top priority targets though it is also realised that preparation will need to be long and thorough. In the meantime highly trained agents, more of them women than men, are being infiltrated into computer centres, first to acquire their stored knowledge and perhaps later to disrupt them.

Chapter Ten

'To entangle the Arab states'

If ever the term 'a love–hate relationship' had a real and literal meaning it must apply to the relations between the PLO and the Arab states. At certain periods great amity has been evident and at other times equal enmity. For long periods both feelings existed simultaneously, with concord on some issues and discord over others. And even during the periods of honeymoon-like reconciliations great suspicion and fear has been apparent on both sides. Mixed with all this has been much self-interest, with each party exploiting the other.

In April 1956, in Cairo, I spent several hours in conversation with President Nasser of Egypt. One topic was the Palestinian refugees, some of whom I had recently seen in Lebanon, and I said that I was surprised that the Arab states had not done more for these unfortunate people.

'The Palestinians are useful to the Arab states as they are,' Nasser said. 'We will always see that they do not become too powerful. Can you imagine yet another nation on the shores of the eastern Mediterranean!'

Nasser was more interested at that time in talking about Britain, Churchill, Eden, himself, Zionism and World War II than about the Palestinians and I could not bring him back to them. I have often regretted this but he had revealed much in his brief comment. His later actions showed that he did indeed regard the Palestinians as useful and he exploited them ruthlessly, seeing to it for his own reasons that they remained poor and destitute; later he would create the PLO for other political ends. All the other Arab states have, in their way, found the PLO as well as the non-PLO Palestinians "useful."

David Hirst, the veteran Middle East correspondent for the *Guardian*, has said, 'The rise of the fedayeen [the Palestinian terrorists] had been an act of Palestinian self-assertion, against the Arabs as well as the Israelis, but, ironically, no sooner had one form of Arab "tutelage" been thrown off than another took its place.'

The analysis of Professor W.F. Abboushi of the creation of Palestinian nationalism, and the role of the Arab states in this is particularly interesting.*

'Palestinian nationalism has developed as a reaction to Arab rejection of the Palestinians,' Professor Abboushi says. 'It was not the result of anything that the Israelis did to the Palestinians. . . . the Arab leaders took from him [the Palestinian] the right to his Arab nationality.'

He makes the point that in 1917, when the British Government issued the Balfour Declaration promising Jews a national home in Palestine there was no Palestine, either in law or in fact. Palestine was a British creation and during the Mandate the Arab people of Palestine thought of themselves are Arabs of southern Syria; their leadership, until 1934, was part of the Syrian Congress.

When in 1948 the Arabs lost the major portions of Palestine they went to the neighbouring countries believing that they were Arabs not Palestinians, according to Abboushi. 'There, their Arab brothers referred to them as "the refugees" and sometimes as "the Palestinians." '

After the 1967 war the Arab people of Palestine began to think of themselves primarily as Palestinians rather than Arabs. The new awareness became almost a new nationalism when King Hussein's government drove them out of Jordan in 1970; the same thing happened during one phase of the Lebanese Civil War, when President Assad's regime

* In *Christian Science Monitor*, January 7, 1980. Abboushi is professor of political science at the University of Cincinnati.

did the same to them. Both Hussein and Assad, in Abboushi's estimate, were "merciless and cruel."

'It became clear that the Arab leaders felt more threatened by the Palestinians than by Israelis. These leaders cultivated parochial feelings among their people to limit their perceived enemy's threat and to stay in power. They made the Palestinians a scapegoat to cover up their incompetence and their failure to transform their societies economically and socially.'

Abboushi draws a parallel between the Zionist idea of a Jewish state and the Palestinians' desire for a state of their own. 'The Palestinians today see the Palestinian state as a refuge from Arab persecution.'

For Abboushi, the analogy does not stop there. The Jews continued to live in the West as influential minorities; so will the Palestinians after the creation of the Palestinian state. 'Both people continue to be envied and sometimes resented in the countries where they live. And both are educated, energetic and goal-oriented.

'Palestinian nationalism is a transient phenomenon,' Abboushi says and claims that it is more of a psychology than a nationalism. If it fails to obtain a Palestinian state, it will return to its Arab origin, but this time it will take on the Arab regimes and resort to violence against "docile" Arabs.

The Arab states want the Palestinians to have a state not so much out of Arab or Islamic brotherhood and unity as from a profound desire to see the PLO and its terrorist groups disappear. The PLO is an irritant; it consumes much of the Arab world's energies and it is dangerously destabilising. It could cause a general war, a civil war or an insurrection at any time and its methods are extreme. Many Arab leaders fear PLO assassination so they buy off this danger by political support within the Middle East and as far afield as the United Nations.

Support for the PLO has become a kind of political rating system. Thus South Yemen is at the top of the table with, usually, Libya and Algeria close behind. At the bottom is Egypt which, paradoxically, has tried harder

129

than any other country to secure a degree of independence for the Palestinians; for years the dispute over autonomy for the Palestinians was the obstacle in the way of full Israeli-Egyptian accord.

The Arab states which helped to bring the PLO into being never gave a thought to the possibility that it could become a force which might turn against them. In 1959 President Nasser's office issued the slogan 'Palestinian entity,' in an attempt to bring about the revival of Palestinism. Nasser believed that he could awaken Palestinian nationalism and make it serve him in his inter-Arab campaigns, which were designed to make Egypt supreme in the Arab world.

Egypt sponsored a group called Organisation for Shattering Refugee Settlement Programmes whose avowed aim was to prevent any attempt to solve the problem of refugees in the countries which had given them sanctuary. Nasser's manoeuvre was purely political and it was at once seen as dangerous by General Qassem of Iraq. Each wanted to use "Palestinian entity" against the other and both wanted to arouse the million Palestinians in Jordan to undermine the Hashemite crown. The setting up of Fatah cells in many cities was partly responsible for the separate efforts by Egypt and Iraq to create their own "Palestinian entity." Jordan took fright and countered the Egyptian and Iraqi moves by offering Jordanian citizenship to Arab Palestinians living outside Jordan's borders.

The Prime Minister, Haze el-Magali, declared: '*We* [the Jordanians] are the army of Palestine; *we* are the refugees." He and his king, Hussein, feared that the kindling of Palestinian nationalistic feelings would endanger the state. Their fears were justified—the Prime Minister was killed by a bomb placed in his desk drawer, allegedly by an Egyptian.

'Palestinian entity' soon involved practically every Arab state and most claimed to have initiated it. Fatah exploited the confusion and the slogan by turning to the Syrians for support; they gave Arafat a headquarters in Damascus and provided training facilities, weapons and money. Nasser had lost control of 'Palestinian entity,' but in 1964, with the founding of the PLO, he saw a chance to restore his declining influence among the Palestinians; he publicly recognised the PLO as playing the role of "vanguard" in the offensive against Israel. But he would direct the vanguard.

Initially Fatah did not join the PLO because its leaders saw that it was an uneasy mixture of factions, each influenced or dominated by Egypt, Iraq, Jordan, Saudi Arabia, Syria and Libya. The heads of these states each feared that the others would use the Arab Palestinian issue to gain prestige and power over his rivals. In a sense Saudi Arabia won the contest since the PLO's first head was Ahmed Shukieri, previously the Saudi representative at the UN. But Nasser soon gained much control by sponsoring the Palestine Liberation Army, a regular, uniformed force, trained by Egyptians in Egyptian territory, Gaza. But Nasser did not have armed conflict in mind and Fatah men believed that the Palestinians would have to spur the Arabs to a war against Israel. When Nasser refused to go to war and fight Israel over Jordan water rights Fatah called the people to revolt against the inactive Arab governments. No immediate revolt was feasible but the threat alarmed Nasser and others; they realised that sooner or later they would have to appease the PLO—since it was now too late to "cancel" it. The Arab states opposed Fatah's first subversive actions. Arab summit meetings and the Arab Unified Command condemned subversive action against Israel for fear of the inevitable retaliation and possibility of war. Jordan and Lebanon even intercepted Fatah raiding parties and arrested them and in some cases shot them.

The PLO made its intentions clear and public. In June 1965 Fatah delegates to the Palestine National Congress in Cairo met the world press for the first time and made a policy statement—their aim was 'to entangle the Arab nations in a war with Israel.' This was too much for Nasser and his associates; they tried to induce Fatah to dissolve itself but even Nasser's personal envoy, the respected

Kamal Rifaat, was rebuffed. Meanwhile the Syrians encouraged the Fatah leadership to operate against Israel from Jordan, in the hope that this would involve Hussein in border conflicts with Israel and weaken his standing among Palestinians living in Jordan. Also, Syria could not then openly be blamed for sabotage acts.

The Arab governments, except Syria, remained anti-Fatah and in January 1966 a meeting of representatives from many of the states issued a warning bulletin: 'The irregular activities conducted by Fatah in the occupied land are ineffective. These operations cause misgivings and the Arab states must beware of them and be on the alert for any information concerning such activities.' The security services of Egypt, Jordan and Lebanon combined to work against Fatah. In May that year even Syria was in conflict with Fatah because it wanted to control Fatah completely; Arafat and his group resisted but it became increasingly difficult for them to operate. Then, with Egypt and Syria collaborating against Jordan, Fatah became useful to both countries for assassination operations.

The defeat of the Arab states in the war of 1967—the Six-Day War—brought the PLO its first opportunity to gain status in the Arab world. With the Arab armies discredited and Nasser's prestige low, there was a vacuum. Fatah and the PLO filled it, claiming an almost messianic role. The rest of the Arab world, not directly in armed conflict with Israel, saw in the PLO a way of restoring Arab pride.

But the PLO has had great difficulty in remaining on even terms with all the Arab states at the one time. This was apparent in December 1980 when Syria and Jordan appeared to be close to war against each other. Jordan was accusing Syria of being anti-Arab because it sided with Iran in its war against Iraq; Syria counter-claimed that Jordan was anti-Islam because it supported Iraq. Arafat, though a strong supporter of Ayatollah Khomeini in Iran, managed not to be drawn into the fierce argument. His policy is much simpler—he supports those who support him and attacks those who are hostile to the PLO. In June

1978 the PLO representative in Kuwait was murdered, apparently by an Iraqi. This led to a burst of violent PLO activity. They attacked the Iraqi mission in Beirut with rockets, bombed the car of the Iraqi ambassador in London and attacked the Iraqi embassy in Paris. On August 3 the PLO representative in Paris was murdered and again the PLO retaliated. This time they blew up a building in Beirut housing the Iraq-backed Palestinian (or Arab) Liberation Front; 98 people died in the collapsing building, yet the PLF is part of the PLO.

Certain Arab states support the PLO for the great advantage it gives them in being able to use the PLO or one of its groups to carry out missions which a government could not do. For instance, Libya, Syria, Algeria, Iraq and Egypt have all at one time or another hired a PLO group to execute a strong-arm mission, to make threats to destabilise a situation or to commit a murder.

Within the Arab world the PLO was given its greatest boost when the Arab League, meeting in Rabat, Morocco, in 1974 recognised the organisation as the sole representative of the Palestinian people' and conferred a 50-million-dollar subsidy. At the same meeting King Hussein bowed to overwhelming pressure and ceded to the PLO "the right" to the West Bank and Arab Jerusalem, which he had lost to the Israelis in the war of 1967.

At Arab summit meetings Arafat, though he does not represent a state, feels no inequality. He acts as if he has special status and frequently insults other delegates. The conference of 50 Arab foreign and economic ministers in Baghdad in March, 1979, was especially noteworthy and is well remembered by those who attended. The main topic was Egypt's peace treaty with Israel. On the first day of the conference Iraq's Saddam Hussein called for the withdrawal of public and private Arab deposits in Egypt and for the freezing of Egypt's membership of inter-Arab organisations and agreements. But the planned easy progression from basic sanctions to a more comprehensive programme was interrupted by an angry intervention from Arafat. He insulted the ministers, one and all, and in particular the Saudi foreign minister, Prince Saud al Faisal. Heady with success from his reception by Khomeini in Iran, Arafat castigated the meeting for not imposing a total economic boycott of Egypt and the USA. He walked out, accompanied by the Libyan and Syrian delegates. The three returned next day for a session of acrimonious exchanges between the Saudis and the Palestinians. Prince Saud accused Arafat of "overbidding" and of theatricals. Arafat told the prince that he was "soft" on those who had killed his father to make a treaty with Israel possible—a reference to the late King Faisal's insistence on the return to Arab sovereignty of Arab Jerusalem.

Furious, Prince Saud threatened to leave for Riyadh. Most of the other delegates also disliked the tone and content of Arafat's remarks. The Kuwaitis acted as mediators and restored a degree of amity. But all meetings attended by Arafat are tense because he quickly flares into anger.

His anger with the Arab states is understandable. While they continue to pay lip service to the ideal of a Palestinian state none of them really wants it to happen. Politically it is better always to be moving towards it than to arrive at it. Without the "legitimate rights of the Palestinians" to fight for there would be much less reason to see Israel as an enemy. Israel as the perceived enemy is the greatest unifying force in the Arab world and the more far-sighted Arab leaders want it to remain so. When the Israelis bombed the nuclear plant near Baghdad in June 1981 the Arab world, though riven with bitter discord, combined to condemn Israel and to threaten retaliation. Even Syria and Jordan temporarily forgot their differences.

Apart from their political need for an external enemy some Arab leaders fear that the Palestinians as a nation would become too powerful and would want to dominate Middle East and Near East politics. In particular the dynastic Arab states—Saudi Arabia, Jordan, Morocco and the Gulf sheikhdoms—fear the powerful Left of the PLO, which hungers for an Arab world revolution as much as it wants to defeat Israel. It is better, most Arab leaders privately say, to keep the Palestinians divided and struggling than to allow them to achieve statehood. The Arab states can safely press for statehood knowing that it is unlikely to happen.

It is useful to show the precise relationship between the PLO and each of the Arab states, with particular reference to points of conflict.

Jordan

Reacting against PLO attempts to take over Jordan, King Hussein fought an internal war against the Palestinians from September 1970 until July 1971, and crushed the terrorists. The Jordanian victory strengthened the Jordanian identification; Palestinians living there were much more "Jordanised" and Jordan became clearly a politically institutionalised entity, while "Palestine" was shown to be an idea, a confused community and factious organisations.

The PLO did not readily accept defeat. In Cairo on November 28, 1971, a hit-team murdered Wasfi el-Tel, the man most responsible for the PLO downfall in Jordan. Having shot him on the steps of the Sheraton Hotel, the killers then drank his blood. In February 1972 a terrorist, at Brunn, near Bonn, West Germany, shot and killed five Jordanians as "traitors." Many other attacks took place, including the attempted assassination of the Jordanian ambassador to London.

King Hussein has repeatedly affirmed the PLO to be "the sole and legitimate representative of the Palestinian people.' In this he is being no more than pragmatic in the interests of his own survival. He would yet again become an assassin's target if he said any less. Yet he can also say, as he did in November 1980 at the Arab summit in Amman, 'We are against attempts at domination of the Palestinian will.'

At other times he has denounced the PLO. 'The PLO as the sole representative of the people of Palestine? Ridiculous! How can half a dozen splintered organisations—partly ruled by criminals who quarrel among themselves about radical ideologies—make such a claim? What they call representation, or war of liberation, is nothing but terror.'*

Earlier, Hussein had protested about the actions of those foreigners who supported the PLO. 'The PLO must not be forced upon the Palestinians, because this people has not yet had a chance to exercise its right to self-determination.'**

In the same interview the king said, 'Developments are moving towards a federation from which a Jordanian-Palestinian entity, with cantons, could emerge.' In this, perhaps, he was close to his own real wishes.

As a pro-PLO Arab nationalist Hussein receives great financial aid from the Arab world. His nation's economy has even benefited from inter-Arab conflicts, such as the Iran-Iraq war. His backing for Iraq has made Jordan a transshipment point for war supplies and consumer goods.

Lebanon

The PLO in Lebanon, reinforced by the arrival of tens of thousands of refugees from Jordan, created a state within a state. After much friction, the PLO and the Lebanese government reached agreement in Cairo. The PLO took over policing and control of all fourteen refugee camps in Lebanon; the government agreed to give the terrorists certain well-defined areas for occupation. The PLO groups gave practically nothing in return beyond promising not to parade the streets of Beirut in full military gear. Tension between the Lebanese and the Palestinians continued and was the fuse which led to the Lebanese War of 1975-76. The detonator was the shooting-up of a Christian funeral party by a gang of PLO terrorists.***

Throughout the 1970s and into the 1980s the PLO clung to their bases in southern Lebanon or "Fatáhland," though often attacked by the Israeli forces. The Lebanese, both Christian and Muslim, are bitter about PLO excesses because Lebanon had done more for the Palestinian

* In the Munich newspaper, *Merkur*, October 28, 1980
** *Zie Zeit*, February 14, 1977
*** The origins and course of the war can be studied in Harald Vocke's book *The Lebanese Civil War*, Hurst and Co., 1978.

refugees than any other country. They blame the PLO for beginning the destruction of Lebanon and Syria for finishing it.

The Israeli invasion of June 1982 was intended to throw both Syria and the PLO out of Lebanon.

Egypt

Egyptian—PLO relations have been marked by sudden about-faces on the part of one side or the other. The government has many times objected to 'Palestinian provocation' leading to riots and murders. When the Egyptians did not condemn Lebanon for trying to curb the excesses of the PLO in 1973 the PLO reaction was bitterly hostile. In that year the Foreign Minister, Zayyat, produced a plan for the creation of a Palestinian state but the PLO rejected it: Such an entity could only be an Egyptian manoeuvre to create a Palestinian authority to negotiate with Israel.

The PLO and many of its influential Western supporters construe President Sadat's actions after the 1973 war against Israel as proving that he did not support the PLO. He agreed, in January 1974, to a first military disengagement and in September 1975 to a second disengagement. He took these steps, under the urging of Dr. Henry Kissinger, to prove that the Egyptian Great Crossing of the Suez Canal was the victory he had claimed it to be, by being magnanimous in victory. President Assad of Syria was furiously angry but he too agreed to a disengagement. These disengagements, as the PLO saw them, were a surrender and sell-out to Israel, largely on Israel's terms, at the very moment when the Egyptians and Syrians should have been pressing their attacks into Israel's heartland. The PLO will never forgive Sadat for this betrayal, which to PLO sympathisers illustrated 'Arab bankruptcy,' to use David Hirst's phrase.

Four PLO terrorists seized the Egyptian Embassy in Madrid on September 15, 1975 and on August 23, 1976 another group hijacked an Egyptian plane en route from Cairo to Luxor.

Sadat's negotiated peace with Israel 1977-78 aroused the PLO to the type of vituperative denunciations generally made against Israelis. The PLO promised immense rewards to anybody who could kill Sadat. In Cyprus PLO terrorists killed one of his closest friends, Youssef Sebai, a newspaper editor, in a bloody incident in Larnaca, in February 1978.

Sadat came in for special hatred when he said, in June 1980, that he no longer agreed with the general Arab view that the PLO is "the sole legitimate representative of the Palestinian people, in the light of its conduct." He was referring to the PLO's foreign policy of violence and its internal one of intimidation. Sadat himself was to become a victim of violence and the PLO applauded his assassination.

Iraq

Iraq's relations with the PLO are dictated by the ruling Ba'ath Party's assessment of its support in Iraq and its conviction that a political settlement with Israel would be a major defeat for the Palestinian cause. The Iraqi administration has consistently aligned itself with the more extreme elements of the PLO. By 1972 friendship was firm and Iraq began to increase its financial aid, it helped to bring the PLO closer to the Soviet Union and it opened Iraqi airports to receive large arms shipments. Later came estrangement and when in 1980 the PLO supported Iran —the enemy of Iraq—this grew into enmity. Nevertheless Iraq retains its links with the 'rejection front,' the more extremist elements of the PLO.

Libya

Libyan involvement with the PLO dates back to the coup d'état which brought Colonel Gaddafi to power in September 1969. Gaddafi saw that to support the PLO would make him a 'progressive' in the eyes of the Arab and Islamic world, and to this end he turned Libya into the terrorists' sanctuary. His relations with the PLO are sometimes difficult; his militant Islamic thinking abhors communist and atheist influences in the PFLP and PDFLP. Nevertheless he allowed Libyans to fight under the banners of Fatah. A breach developed because Gaddafi constantly hectored the PLO chiefs and at one time, in 1973, relations were disrupted. In December 1979 Gaddafi broke with Arafat on the grounds that the PLO was 'selling out' the Palestinian people; Arafat was wasting his time, in Gaddafi's opinion, by touring the world for diplomatic support when he should be fighting. He urged the PLO to blow up the Suez Canal and the oil fields be handed over by Israel to Egypt.

Gaddafi kept the PLO staff in Tripoli imprisoned in their headquarters and expelled Farouk Khaddoumi, then in Libya. The row came to an end when Gaddafi realised that he needs the PLO as much as they need Libyan money. Having sentenced to death those Libyans living abroad who would not obey his order to return, Gaddafi wanted experienced terrorists to carry out his threats.

Saudi Arabia

The PLO's relations with this "reactionary" regime have been ambiguous. Initially Saudi Arabia was friendly to Fatah because a militant Palestinian group with leaders opposed to Nasserism deserved to be encouraged. But the relationship soured as the Saudis became aware of PFLP and PDFLP plans to overthrow the Saudi monarchy. Then Black September stormed the Saudi embassy in Khartoum in May 1973 and held the ambassador and several diplomatic guests hostage—and murdered some of them. A further rift followed when Salah Khalaf visited South Yemen—Saudi Arabia was virtually at war with South Yemen—and promised PLO support for 'the struggle of the Yemeni people for liberation from [Saudi Arabian] imperialism.'

Arafat's personal diplomacy brought a form of recognition which became official when Saudi Arabia agreed, at the Algiers Arab summit in November 1973, to support the PLO as the sole representative of the Palestinian people. In 1980 the Saudis gave the PLO a present of 40 million dollars; this was an investment to buy off the PLO from becoming involved in any plan to depose the monarchy.

Sudan

The PLO alienated President Numeiri of the Sudan when a gang butchered two American diplomats and a Belgian in the Saudi embassy in March 1973. The furious president, formerly a PLO supporter, announced that he saw 'no heroism' in the exploit and criticised the Fatah men for inhumanity. Students of Khartoum university, usually pro-PLO, joined in their president's denunciation. 'Can any sane mind justify the outrage?' one of their posters demanded to know. The head and deputy head of the Fatah bureau in Khartoum had planned the deed—an abuse of Sudanese hospitality. Nevertheless Sudan supports the PLO, if only as a form of insurance to protect itself from further outrage.

Kuwait

Kuwait has always tried to play the part of the neutral state accommodating Arab and international viewpoints and reconciling the differences between the Arab regimes. It also has a large Palestinian community. The PLO has been careful to cultivate the friendship of Kuwait, despite its status as a conservative regime. Like Saudi Arabia, Kuwait objected at first to the legitimization of the PLO's claim to be the sole representative of the Palestinians. And, like Saudi Arabia, Kuwait has had to put up with terrorist operations aimed at least partly against itself; the PFLP occupied the Japanese Embassy in Kuwait to secure the release of prisoners taken in a Singapore incident. Neither Kuwait nor the inherently conservative Palestinian community have shown much sympathy for the PLO.

Bahrein, Qatar and Oman

All have been on bad terms with the PLO because of the subversive activities of some of its groups.

140

The Mahgreb

The three Western Arab states have had varied experience with the PLO. Morocco and the PLO have a reciprocal detestation and the PLO regards King Hassan as "the pawn of imperialism;" in February 1974 Black September made an assassination attempt on his life during the Arab summit. In contrast, Algeria, itself the child of a revolution, is one of the PLO's main backers, while Tunisia has tried to pay lip service to the "Palestinian cause" while remaining otherwise uninvolved. The PLO would much like to see Tunisia become more militant and its agents have been working towards this end since 1971. The PLO was then interfering in Tunisian affairs and calling for the overthrow of what they termed "the fascist regime" of President Bourguiba. A joint statement signed by all the major groups charged the Tunisian government with masterminding the murder in Beirut of the Arab Liberation Front's leader, Ibrahim Sukeimi.

South Yemen

This is the one Arab country where the PLO is accepted without reserve. The country is a Soviet satellite and any revolutionary movement can find a base there and participate in the country's main industry, the training of terrorists and subversives. The government is in no way threatened by the PLO which has no interest in local politics. Similarly, the government does not concern itself with the PLO's activities. Because of its virtually inpenetrable security South Yemen is the PLO's safest haven.

As for the future, the country most inextricably entangled with the PLO's affairs is Jordan. This was ensured by one of President Sadat's terms for his peace treaty with Israel—that there be autonomy for the Palestinians. Because of popular world support for a Palestinian state, Jordanian nationalism and Palestinian nationalism have become impacted. The result is what the Israelis call 'the Jordanian option.' This would allow the West Bank to be re-absorbed or federate with Jordan. Hussein has shown no great liking for this option. He fears the radical West Bank state as much as Israel does, especially if it came to him with the PLO attached. Nor does King Hussein favour the idea of a Palestinian state formed by linking Gaza and the West Bank. If it were controlled by the PLO he would be vulnerable to PLO expansionism—that is bringing into the new state the great number of Palestinians living in Jordan.

As the Israelis see the Jordanian option, Israel and Jordan would bypass the PLO and negotiate directly over the future of the West Bank. It would be a way of avoiding a PLO-dominated state on the West Bank. For his part Hussein would get a limited amount of territory returned directly to him to become part of Jordan.

The option is, strictly speaking, not an option at all but an obligation. In subscribing to the UN's resolution 242 after the 1967 war, the Hashemite kingdom undertook to settle peacefully its dispute with Israel. That means, primarily drawing up by agreement a frontier of secure peace between the two countries. Jordan's imprint has long been evident in almost everything that happens on the West Bank. The Israelis say that if Amman is truly unwilling to discuss anything other than the return of every single square inch of Israel-held territory it should be prepared to cease daily involvement in West Bank affairs.

The PLO claims a Jordanian option. Farouk Khaddoumi has said that 'there should be a kind of linkage between a Palestinian mini-State and Jordan because Jordanians and Palestinians are considered by the PLO as one people.' King Hussein worries about the implications of such 'linkage', though statistically Khaddoumi's notion of 'one people' carries some weight. In Amman 85 per cent of the population is Palestinian; banking, commerce and industry are in the hands of Palestinians and the civil service is virtually run by Palestinians. King Hussein

142

allows only four Palestinians in his cabinet, a quota which makes a coup inside the government practically impossible. Otherwise only in the armed forces are Palestinians in a minority and under control.

The PLO undoubtedly has its moderates but the man who dares to reveal moderate views runs great dangers, even outside the Arab world. A noted moderate, Said Hammami, the PLO representative in London, was murdered on January 4, 1978. Hammami had proposed co-existence with Israel and for this heresy was 'executed', probably by an Iraqi terrorist.

Despite assassinations, political pressure and even wars of extermination, President Nasser in his time and all the other Arab leaders since have failed to prevent the Palestinians of the PLO from becoming 'too powerful.' Hussein cut away their power in Jordan but they became even more powerful in Lebanon. The number of offices the PLO civil servants moved into in Amman, Damascus and Beirut was remarkable and the PLO presence is ubiquitous. I have seen their vehicles, packed with armed men, patrolling city streets as casually as street vendors. In leading hotels and restaurants every Western journalist assigned to the Middle East would recognise senior terrorists entertaining foreign visitors. Expensive apartments are adorned with fiery posters and slogans, as frequently directed against Arab governments as against the Israelis. President Assad of Syria perceived that the PLO was 'too powerful' in Lebanon, and for a time during the Lebanese War the world saw the astonishing spectacle of the Syrian Army fighting with the Christian forces *against* the Palestinians. Once the PLO had been reduced in power and prestige the Syrians changed allegiances.

Like President Nasser in 1956 other Arab leaders are not enchanted by the idea of yet another nation on the shores of the Eastern Mediterranean, especially when it would have sizeable, intelligent, educated minorities living as a diaspora within the larger Arab world. 'The PLO,' a former Egyptian Prime Minister told me, 'are the malcontents of the Middle East.'

Malcontents are disruptive and must be kept in check. 'All the peace-seeking Arab regimes share the same strategic purpose,' says David Hirst, 'they all want to cut the Palestinians down to size.'

To this end, every Arab state has infiltrated its own agents into the PLO groups and their overseas branches. While professing support for the PLO the Arab leaders do not really trust the organisation. Many are jealous of Arafat's prestige; Gaddafi is the prime example. As he tells friends, he is unwelcome in most of the world's capitals though he personally has never killed anybody—a claim that is probably true—while Arafat, Gaddafi alleges, is a multiple murderer. Arab generals, too, are envious of the advanced weapons available to the Palestinians which they themselves cannot acquire.

Some of the PLO's terror groups have profoundly alienated Arab society, particularly in Jordan. The PDFLP broadcast Marxist slogans from a mosque minaret to commemorate Lenin's birth, an affront to Islam. And it became known that PDFLP members were visiting the tents of Jordanian women by night for illicit sex. For many Jordanians, Palestinian as well as Bedouin, the PDFLP terrorists were not only blasphemers but degenerates.

The 'popular' support which the PLO claims to have is largely the type of support that comes from the fear *not* to support; partly it stems from the resigned awareness that better leadership is not available.

The PLO leaders in Beirut and Damascus are wary of granting West Bank Palestinians more power than they already have for fear of what they refer to as *qiyada badilla* —substitute leadership. This was obvious in mid-1980 after certain West Bankers formed a National Guidance Committee. Though PLO supporters they were critical of some actions by the PLO and spoke out against them. The unofficial chairman of the Committee, Bassam Shak'a, was summoned to Amman where one of Arafat's deputies told him to 'think again' about the need for a National Guidance Committee. Would it not be better to leave guidance to the PLO? That the PLO could virtually dictate to Shak'a, the highly regarded mayor of Nablus, shows the organisation's power.

Popular mistrust of the PLO has been noticed by several observers. David Pryce-Jones is typical:

'What is brutally exposed is the absence of a PLO base among the Palestinian masses. The PLO is expressed not as a national movement but as a series of intricate in-fights among a few personalities, who become ever more unscrupulous as they lose their toe-holds in one Arab capital after another. In national conflicts, as between Iraq and Iran, or Iran and Syria, the PLO is an interloper, its interests only those Arafat declares them to be.'*

Ordinary Palestinians cannot express themselves in political terms about the PLO and its role in their lives. For them life is a basic matter of survival. In the village of Beni Naim, near Hebron, I interviewed Muhammad Housein Zaidat, a young West Banker, in his typically plain and simple but comfortable Arab house. As we sat on mattresses on the floor, Zaidat told me that he had joined Fatah to fight as a terrorist because the only alternative open to him at the time was to enlist in the Jordanian Army—and Fatah paid better wages. He found Fatah life too violent and he surrendered to the Israelis; he was briefly imprisoned before returning to his village, where his experiences had made him respected. He was afraid of Fatah's long arm of retribution. He said, 'They are bastards and they will want revenge because I surrendered to the Israelis.' He was right. They did. Zaidat was killed a few years later.

PLO hatred of fellow-Arabs seen to be friendly with Jews is implacable and operates across borders. Some PLO members, looking from the Lebanon frontier straight into an Israeli village, noted that one Arab girl frequently visited a Jewish family. One day her friends

* In *The New Republic*, December 1980.

found her stabbed to death; her naked body had been flung across a dunghill.

Other really moderate Palestinians have paid for their moderation with their lives. One victim, in November 1980, was Muhammad Abu-Warda, a leading supporter of the Egyptian peace initiative. A prominent politician and deputy chairman of the local council of Jabalya camp, north of Gaza, Abu-Warda travelled with bodyguards but a terrorist shot him at point-blank range and escaped. Abu-Warda was a member of the first delegation of Gaza notables to visit Egypt after Sadat's trip to Jerusalem. Another member of the delegation was murdered in 1978. In PLO circles Abu-Warda was considered one of the main collaborators with Israeli authorities and calls for his assassination had been broadcast for some time by the PLO radio station.

Housein Zaidat, Abu-Warda and the friendly Arab girl were victims of the organisation which had set out many years before to give them a voice. In 'entangling the Arab nations'—its declared aim—it had lost its way.

Chapter Eleven

'A new kind of militant'

'We have to train a totally new kind of militant,' George Habash told me in Beirut in 1972. 'What the PFLP and all the other PLO groups need is revolutionary awareness.' His new kind of militant fighter would have fervour, dedication, ruthlessness and education.

There was nothing new in the history of militancy about the first three of his requirements but education—in the way that Habash meant it—was certainly new. It was to be an education based on indoctrination and on creating an intellectual understanding of the revolutionary ideal.

'The PFLP is fighting imperialism, Zionism and Arab reaction,' Habash said, and after a long discussion about these three 'great evils' he summed up the PFLP's attitude in this way:

'We are struggling against imperialism, especially the American form of it, in as much as it is the brake on any real development for the Arab societies which are essentially wholly dependent upon it.

'We are struggling against Zionism—and therefore Israel—which is an ally of imperialism and, we feel, its major ally in the Middle East.

'We are struggling against Arab reaction—you will know the long list of countries I could name—because the governing classes in our countries are either involved in imperialism or are quite incapable of solving the vital problems of our societies.'

Education of the new militant revolutionary was needed

if he was to understand the complexity of the revolution and thus take his proper place in it, Habash explained. Education in the PFLP training camps at that time was thorough, as I was able to observe for myself at Habash's main training camp about 30 miles from Amman. It covered a vast area and had individual hiding places scattered all over it, in case of emergency. During the Jordanian attempt to wipe out the terrorists many PFLP men used these hiding places and later escaped by night.

During my visit to the PFLP school the course lasted five months, longer than those run by other movements. The training given, both political and military, was directed to forming cadres capable of running bases, creating and giving purpose to clandestine cells and planning guerrilla action in town and country.

The programme was based on 45 hours of work per week, with political and military studies alternating from week to week. The political programme was divided into four sections with courses made up of factual lectures, explanations and discussion of books. The status of teachers varied; some had come to give only one lecture and depart while others were paid staff. The students, aged from 18 to 30, were carefully selected and their programme covered these subjects:

1 *Marxist-Leninist theory:*
   Principles of Marxist philosophy
   The Communist Manifesto
   Marx, Engels, Marxism, Lenin
   Utopian socialism and scientific socialism
   State and revolution
   Origins of the family, the state and property
2 *The kind of age we are living in:*
   Imperialism
   Revolution and counter-revolution
   National liberation movements and neo-colonialism
   The Socialist Camp and the Third World
   The revolution in China, Korea, Vietnam and Cuba
   The workers' movement in Europe

The National Arab Liberation Movement
Arab unity and socialist perspectives
3 *Political problems:*
Israel and what it is like
Imperialism and the Arab reaction
The strategy of the war for popular liberation
The nature of the regimes in Jordan, Lebanon, Syria,
    Iraq, Egypt
The Palestinian problem and the Arab world
4 *PFLP:*
The birth and development of the movement
The first split and its causes (PFLP—High Command)
The second split and its causes (PDFLP)
The PFLP as the Marxist-Leninist Party
The PFLP at the military level
Relations with political organisations and the Arab
    states
The PFLP in Lebanon
The PFLP and the Arab Nationalist Movement

The programme included daily physical training, practice in close combat fighting, and day and night marches.
There were classes in strategy and tactics of guerrilla
warfare, and on significant chapters from the works of
Clausewitz, Mao and Giap. Instruction was given in the
use of heavy and light arms—the equipment being Russian, American and Israeli. Several courses covered the
Israeli army and its methods.

Courses have changed little except in producing even
more radical graduates. Ghassan Kanafani, one of the
main planners of the PFLP school's syllabus, told me in
1972: 'There are now only a few hundred Palestinians
dedicated to revolution but they are the catalyst which will
produce the Arab revolution. There is much more to it
than anti-Zionism. After the internal social and cultural
revolutions the Arab world must confront the United
States.'

He was prepared to manipulate endlessly and the conflict with Israel was his way of life. Reverses depressed him

at what he called his 'emotional level' but his ideology and dedication were impervious to them. He had more of a pathological hatred for the Jews than other leading terrorists had—and an equal hatred for 'that shit' Hussein. The revolution for which he was planning would, in the end, remove all the Arab monarchs of whatever rank. Because the monarchs would naturally try to preserve their feudal and corrupt regimes, he said, 'Black September was logical. There could be ten Black Septembers.'

Kanafani told me wrily that he was grateful for the existence of Israel because only opposition to Israel could rouse the Arab masses from their apathy sufficiently to set off the Arab-world revolution. In his office he had some notable souvenirs—the coat of arms of the American Embassy in Amman and of the Jordanian Embassy in Beirut, both stolen during riots. Marxist, Che Guevara and Mao posters adorned the walls of his office and mortar bombs were holding down papers on the shelves.

When I commented on the children being innocent and uncomprehending victims of the Middle East turmoil Kanafani was impatient. 'There are no innocents,' he said. 'If you are alive you're involved. Innocence is meaningless. It's not logical for any person to expect to be excluded from social struggle on the grounds of age or sex or anything else. Palestinian children can expect no favours. In fact, they are privileged; they are the ones who will carry through the revolution, not those of my generation. What does the life of an Arab child or a Jewish child matter if their death will help bring about the revolution?'

Bassam Abou Sharif, aged 29, who succeeded Kanafani as PFLP spokesman, was injured and blinded by a parcel bomb explosion; while he was recovering in hospital somebody sent him poisoned sweets. Since Sharif was in no way implicated in the Tel Aviv airport massacre it must be assumed that the Israelis were not responsible for the attempts on his life despite the allegations that they had killed Kanafani.

Kanafani had told me, 'Life tends to be precarious for some of us,' and I am reminded of this whenever I pass the spot where he died. I had reason to think of him in August 1980 when I was in Beirut. On this occasion I had taken with me to Lebanon a Herefordshire corn-dolly, an artistic design in corn using stalks and grain and made as a symbol of the harvest and fertility. It was intended as a gift for a family from Ashrafiya I have known for many years. I found that since my previous visit the war had driven them out to the poor suburb of Dorah. The mother, Katerina, received the dolly emotionally. It was, she said, such a peaceful, civilised gift and she was overcome by its purity, such a contrast to the barbarity of Lebanon. She put it on a ribbon and looped it around her neck. 'It will be something to remember you by,' she said.

In 1980 Lebanon had become a dangerous place for journalists and writers; many have been threatened, kidnapped or murdered. The Sunni Muslim editor Salim El Laouzi was found with his tongue torn out and a hand cut off, an Islamic punishment for those who sin by what they say or write. El Laouzi had criticised the Syrians and Palestinians for their cruelty. The BBC and Reuters correspondents had been driven out by threats.

Barbarism has destroyed this beautiful land right down to its core. Physical destruction is most evident in Beirut. I found one family of old friends living in one habitable room and a cellar and sleeping on mattresses on the floor. Public services are intermittent and though these people have a telephone they know it is tapped. The boys of the family go to school by day—when it is safe for the school to open—and at night they are in the 'front-line'. The shops close at sundown and the streets are empty by early evening. Everywhere there is wreckage, the burnt-out hulks of buildings, expanses of wasteland. Gardens are untended and this once beautiful city is desolate.

There has been destruction too of a once tolerant and civilised way of life, and of people's personalities. They have been terribly changed by a war which has gone on since 1975. All the people I met are nervous and tense and at the slightest unusual noise after dark they reach for their weapons. If shooting starts they quickly get under cover.

'Oh God,' they say wearily. 'Who is it this time?' They mean does the threat come from the Syrian Army—the so-called peacekeeping force—from the Palestinians or some other attacker.

People have banded into many groups as a form of survival. When I was there a new group emerged—the Front for the Liberation of Lebanon From Foreigners, meaning the Syrians and Palestinians. I have sympathy for their desperation if not for the means they use to get foreigners out, such as booby-traps in cars.

Some of the new fighting in Lebanon in 1980-81 was between supporters of Iraq and Iran—Sunni Muslims backing Iraq and Shi'ites backing Iran. This was another layer of conflict laid on top of all the others. The PLO has created great problems. Despite the presence of the United Nations force the PLO is continually active, striking either at the Christians or into Israel. Under Soviet and Syrian instigation, the PLO is eager to rekindle the Southern Lebanon front as a kind of radiation centre, hoping that from here conflict will spread still further. Significantly the battle cry of armed Muslims fighting the Christians is now 'Din al Islam aqwa'—the faith of Islam is stronger.

Before I left Beirut to return home I went to Dorah to visit Katerina and her family. The family was in mourning. Katerina had been killed the previous night, hit by a burst of bullets fired through her kitchen window while she prepared a meal. Her daughter handed me the corn-dolly, stained with blood, and said, 'So that you can remember my mother.'

The bullets had been fired, according to local report, by Palestinians in a passing vehicle. Nobody can be sure as Syrian soldiers could have fired those shots. For Ghassan Kanafani, killed at a spot not far away eight years before, the identity of the assassin would be of no consequence; what matters is that he had advanced the revolution a further step. The slaughter in Lebanon—with perhaps as many as 75,000 dead since 1975—would prove to Kanafani that the Arab world is in the throes of the revolution he so desperately wanted.

But the revolution has had profound effects far beyond the Arab world. The methods of the revolution, principally terror, have been exported to every continent. Through its multi-faceted activities, all intensively pursued, the PLO has brought about significant changes in outlook, if not directly then through the many national terrorist groups which have copied it and probably have been trained by it. Terrorism has shaped people's attitudes to violence as a form of political expression, to justice, to authority, even to the values of life and death. By the PLO's own figures, it carried out 10,000 operations between 1967 and the end of 1980.* Such saturation terrorism has the effect of making terrorism appear normal. In operations aimed at Israel the PLO has not achieved its short-term aims, such as release of PLO prisoners, nor has it noticeably weakened Israeli resolve, but they greatly encouraged the terrorist organisations of Spain, Ireland, Italy, West Germany, Holland, Japan and South America. To be as operationally effective as the PLO became the ambition of most other groups.

Most revolutionary and terrorist organisations project an image of persecution and impoverishment. The PLO, in contrast, is a de luxe terror group. Uniquely, it does not operate on the run and is neither persecuted nor impoverished; it operates from office blocks with a paid staff working regular hours, taking annual holidays and receiving PLO pensions. Because of the extensive aid it receives from the Arab States and from the Soviet Union and the bases at its disposal it is strong financially and politically, with an income of at least £1,000 million a year. Its extensive infrastructure is its main attraction for the world's underground movements; many would wither away without PLO support.

The greatest change in international public perception

---

* Other figures: The Israelis suffered 640 people killed and 3,424 injured, most of them civilians. In 1980 9 Israeli soldiers and 19 settlers were killed, 58 soldiers and 77 settlers wounded. *The Palestine Report*, January 1981.

of the PLO occurred when Arafat mounted the rostrum at the United Nations to become the only non-government leader, apart from the Pope, to address the General Assembly. Until this point people had no problem recognising terrorism. After Arafat appeared at the UN a change occurred. Many people began to wonder if what they had assumed to be terrorism was not, after all, terrorism. Or perhaps there was such a thing as justifiable terrorism. At the very least, values became confused.

Arafat's 100 minutes at the UN rostrum also changed the nature of the UN itself. It became a theatre rather than a debating chamber. Habash, Kanafani, Arafat and many others had always known that theatre is the priceless asset of terrorism. It is immensely absorbing to the vast majority of people whose lives are not directly touched by it. One of the first PLO supporters to see this was Soraya Antonius, to whom I have already referred. 'We found that when we picked up a gun people wanted to talk with us,' she said.

Hundreds of journalists wanted to interview PLO chiefs and record their views for radio and press, to film them for television. In many countries embryo terrorists and disaffected people saw the publicity benefits of killing policemen, politicians and judges in the name of a revolutionary cause, in planting bombs, in taking over an embassy, in holding hostages, in carrying out a massacre. The greatest coup, since it led to the widest media coverage, was the aerial hijack, a form of piracy. The media of every country in the world reported the PFLP's mass hijack, in July 1970, of planes owned by Swissair, BOAC, TWA, Pan American and El Al. Four of the planes went up in flames —three in Jordan and one in Egypt. It is true that some PFLP leaders had not wanted to destroy them but to use them for bargaining with Israel. Militants thought this was weakness. This difference was typical of the gulf between the academic moderates and the rejectionists who favour direct and ruthless action. This episode, and others, show that terrorism cannot be controlled. Logically, it becomes bigger than its creators. In the thinking of Kanafani and other intellectuals—and in Arafat's mind by 1976—this was as it should be. If you train men in ruthlessness you cannot then expect them to show 'moderation.' Moderation is meaningless in revolution. It implies compromise and no revolution ever succeeded with compromise.*

This point is missed by those well-meaning Western people who ask the PLO to recognise the right of Israel to exist. Such a request is based on the assumption that the PLO's *sole* desire is to achieve an independent state of its own. The majority of its influential members want much more than this; they want revolution and to recognise Israel would abort the revolution. If they acknowledge Israel then Israel must perforce acknowedge the PLO —and the Arab revolution would wither from lack of nourishment.

Because PLO pressure is insistent and its presence ubiquitous the organisation cannot be ignored. It is like a nagging toothache; one can tolerate the irritation for only so long before 'doing something' about it. The European initiative is a way of 'doing something' about the PLO. The Western wish to see that the PLO is treated 'justly' may have less to do with justice than with a fervent desire to be rid of the PLO's attentions.

PLO influence, power and prestige are largely the result of the ubiquitous nature of the movement. By 1980 it had offices in 82 countries; in 1981 the Soviet Union gave it a tremendous boost by giving the PLO agent in Moscow ambassadorial status. In that year too the British Foreign Secretary, in his role as chairman of the European Council of Foreign Ministers, met Arafat—another boost. Long before that the Foreign Office had been holding regular meetings with the PLO's London representative, Nabil

---

* In 1976 the US Foreign Affairs Committee of the United States House of Representatives met to consider 'the problem of the Palestinians.' Among the many witnesses were two PLO spokesmen, both academics and regarded as moderate, Professor Edward Said and Professor Abu Lughod. Both evaded questions about the PLO's intentions towards Jordanian and Israeli territory and whether the PLO would recognise Israel if Israel agreed to recognise the Palestinians' right to self-determination.

Ramlawi; he was invited, on a regular basis, to meet senior Foreign Office officials at the FO itself, tacit recognition of status.

The contents of any one issue of *Palestine*, the PLO information bulletin, shows the worldwide nature of the organisation. Here are headlines from the issue of April 1-15, 1981:

ARAFAT PARTICIPATES IN BANGLADESH IN-DEPENDENCE CELEBRATIONS

FAROUK KHADDOUMI MEETS CARDINAL CASAROLI IN VATICAN

ARAFAT RECEIVES US PROTESTANT CHURCH DELEGATION

EFFORTS TO END GULF WAR CONTINUED IN TEHERAN AND BAGHDAD

CHAIRMAN ARAFAT VISITS YEMEN ARAB RE-PUBLIC

ARAFAT MEETS SAUDI KING

FAROUK KHADDOUMI MEETS TUNISIAN PRE-MIER

PLO RECEIVES MESSAGE FROM SOVIET LEAD-ERSHIP

FAROUK KHADDOUMI INAUGURATES ARAB-MALTESE FRIENDSHIP SOCIETY

PALESTINIAN CULTURAL ACTIVITIES IN TURKEY

BULGARIAN COMMUNIST PARTY SUPPORT FOR PLO

The preceding issue carried reports of Arafat 'receiving' the Rumanian foreign minister, Iranian delegations and an Italian delegation. He congratulated King Juan Carlos on the failure of the military uprising and the Mongolian president on the occasion of the 60th anniversary of the foundation of the Mongolian Revolutionary Party.

PLO propaganda has generated a momentum for 'the Palestinian problem' which, apparently, cannot be checked. This was vividly shown in September 1980 when the International Monetary Fund and the World Bank held their joint annual meeting in Washington. Serious disagreement arose over, of all things, the PLO. *The Economist* reported:*

> That ritual debating society motion—Should the PLO attend international meetings as an observer? —has been stupidly allowed to acquire real financial significance. Let the PLO in, and the American Congress has vowed that it will cut American contributions to both bodies. [World Bank and IMF] Keep the PLO out, and several oil-rich Arab states will not lend directly to the IMF . . . The PLO issue has whiskers. It was raised in earnest last year, which should have given sensible people plenty of time to persuade finance ministers, especially those from developing countries, that Palestine and the world's monetary system are separate subjects, and that keeping them separate does not mean compromising one's Palestinian sympathies.

During 1981 the PLO launched a major propaganda campaign on the theme of 'solidarity', the idea being to induce foreign revolutionary movements to declare their solidarity with the PLO. This was at once successful. In one week during February the Unified Union of Chilean Workers, the People's Republic of Vietnam, the Vietnamese National Liberation Front and the Moroccan National Students' Association all proclaimed solidarity. The dedicated effort with which such proclamations are sought must be admired. For instance, the PLO representative in Paris heard that the Union of Chilean Workers in France was organising a festival to celebrate the 29th Anniversary of the Union. Trained to exploit such occasions, he lobbied Chilean officials and induced them to make the occasion a 'festival of solidarity' with the Palestinian people. It was held in the Mutualité Hall, Paris, on Friday February 20. Song and dance troupes from France, Algeria and Chile took part and Musa Jreis, representative of

* September 27, 1980

the general secretariat of the Lebanon branch of the Palestinian Union of Workers, a PLO offshoot, made a speech. It was an impressive address, well delivered, and based on what Jreis called 'the conspiracies against the Palestinian Revolution by Zionist, imperialist and reactionary forces.' He conveyed to the Chilean workers best wishes from Chairman Arafat and the Palestinian freedom fighters and pointed out that Palestinians and Chileans had much in common. 'We are two peoples united against imperialism, Zionism and Fascism,' he said. Speakers from the Chilean Union of Workers and the French General Confederation of Workers, historically sensitive to conspiracies, fervently promised Jreis their support and solidarity. When journalists spoke to Comrade Navaro, of the Chilean Workers' Union, after the meeting it was clear that he believed that Palestine had some geographical and political connection with *Pakistan*. 'The Zionists of Pakistan must let Palestine go,' he said sincerely and meaninglessly.

At meetings such as that in Paris it is PLO practice to try to induce the leading speakers not only to express solidarity with the Palestinian struggle but to accept leadership of the PLO in this undertaking. This gives the PLO an important psychological advantage when they come to make further requests of the allied organisation.

Propaganda coups are now commonplace, especially for Arafat; in his distinctive costume he is a good draw and can be counted on to inject some controversy into what might otherwise be a dull meeting. His secretariat works hard to obtain invitations to conferences, particularly those in which the PLO can show its non-terrorist face. A meeting for which Arafat had great hopes was the 1980 annual UNESCO conference in Belgrade, which he was invited to address. He concluded his lecture with a call for solidarity among the struggling peoples of the world. 'The Palestinian Revolution is in the mainstream of the universal struggle for progress, democracy and justice,' he said.

Expert lobbying brought Israel under repeated criticism throughout the UNESCO conference. The Culture and

Communications Commission adopted a resolution 'vigorously condemning' Israel for its policy on Jerusalem. The resolution noted that the latest decision to make Jerusalem its eternal capital 'modified the character and status of the holy city of Jerusalem and is yet another of the many obstacles placed by Israel in the way of UNESCO's continuing its efforts to protect the common heritage of mankind.' This is almost word for word from PLO leaflets distributed months before the conference. The UNESCO Education Commission passed another resolution—89 votes to 18 with 10 abstentions—against Israel's education policy in the Israeli-administered territories.

Such intensive anti-Israel activity makes the Israelis more stubborn in their insistence that they will not 'sit down at the same table' with the PLO.

No major conference, on whatever subject, is considered irrelevant by the PLO. For the first time, in 1981, a representative attended a world tourism conference in Manila as 'official observer.' The purpose in attending was ostensibly to advise about tourism in the Arab countries. In fact, the PLO man was briefed on how to get across two false messages—that Israel does not welcome tourists and that service is bad in all respects. He was also to warn that there was the danger that freedom fighters from the West Bank and Gaza might plant bombs in public buses. Because Israel is well established as a tourist attraction it is doubtful if the PLO's campaign had any success but it was enough for the PLO that it had been seen to attend the conference. Each such occasion adds to the propaganda momentum and provides further credibility for the PLO's non-terrorist face.

Until about 1975 PLO terrorism was deplored and condemned by national leaders. Gradually, as violence against established institutions became more commonplace, international reaction dropped 'deplore' and 'condemn' from its vocabulary. The adjectives 'shocking' and 'terrible' and the noun 'atrocity' have also gone or are fading away. At most a terrorist attack can be called 'bloody' because it generally is. Not that world leaders praise PLO terrorism—or that committed by any other group; most have terrorism within their own borders. But it is no longer a phenomenon; it is accepted as normal—as normal as violent death in Lebanon. It might not be excused but an explanation is found for it. 'An oppressed people must be expected to react angrily.' This is increasingly the case with reactions to PLO terrorism, and it is a logical development of the reception of Yasser Arafat at the United Nations. Nobody wants to admit that a man received into the General Assembly is a terrorist or that he represents a terrorist organisation. Arafat might not fit Habash's description of a 'new kind of militant' but he has imparted to violence a new kind of respectability, and it is accepted by the world with a new kind of resignation.

Chapter Twelve

The PLO Disconnection

There is a natural tendency in the West to regard the PLO as a political group in the way that the British Labour Party is a party, at whose meetings members may publicly put forward their views no matter how much they may offend other members of the party. In the end by a process of debate, compromise and vote a consensus will emerge. The PLO does not function in this way; consensus is an irrelevance except in the narrow sense in which agreement is reached by the ruling triumvirate of Arafat, Khalil al-Wazir (Abu Jihad) and Salah Khalaf (Abu Iyad).

Arafat is the world traveller and the public figure, continually appearing on the international stage; the world has drawn the conclusion that he is the policy-maker of the PLO. But back in Beirut and in other capitals are a dozen PLO barons and none more powerful than al-Wazir and Khalaf, neither of whom appear in the West. They, too, are policy-makers.

The future course of the PLO will be shaped by the relationship of Arafat and these two. In the 1980s a split is emerging which may be irreparable. Superficially, the reasons for the split are tactical. Arafat and al-Wazir think that it would be politically expedient, for a time at least, to cease activities against Israeli objectives, especially those outside Israel. Khalaf, the former head of the Black September organisation, believes otherwise.

The real reasons for the division lie deeper, and are to be found in the personalities and the personal relations of the three as much as in their different perceptions of how to advance the Palestinian cause.

Khalaf is an interesting man and a frightening one. Born in Gaza in 1930, he went to Cairo University in 1950 but spent more time as a Palestinian activist than at his studies. With Arafat and al-Wazir he was arrested for associating with the anti-Nasser Muslim Brotherhood and banished. The three men laid the foundations of Fatah, with Khalaf living mostly in Damascus, concentrating on terrorism against Israel through Jordan and the West Bank. In 1968 he was appointed chief of intelligence and became in effect Arafat's deputy. He was Fatah's representative to the Palestinian National Council and responsible for developing international contacts. His real rise came with the disclosure that he was head of Black September, the terrorist unit responsible for the Olympic Games massacre in 1972. In 1975 he was given one of the most important PLO positions—head of internal security. This gave him the power to order the death of any member.

Liking the high life, Khalaf drinks heavily, is notorious as a womaniser and is reputed to be one of the best organisers of orgies in the Middle East. His colleagues deplore his personal habits but they dare not protest.

Alarmed by Khalaf's use of the power they had given him, Arafat and al-Wazir plotted against him. Having moved Khalaf's key agents to other sectors of the PLO, Arafat and al-Wazir prepared the ground for stripping him of his important posts during the May 1980 Palestinian National Congress meeting. He lost his job as head of internal security and as chief of intelligence.

In most political organisations, that would have been the end of Khalaf as an active force. But in the PLO none of the officials has been elected, and none is responsible to Palestinian constituents. Each member of the triumvirate has an alliance with a different segment of the Arab world, which uses the PLO as an extension of its own national goals.

The PLO is thus a microcosm of inter-Arab rivalry. Far

from neutralising Khalaf, Arafat achieved the opposite, for neither he nor al-Wazir had predicted the outbreak of Iraqi-Iranian hostilities, an event which enabled Khalaf to exploit the inner workings of the PLO to his advantage. He managed to retain his position in the hierarchy and to align himself openly with the anti-Arafat forces in the Arab world, the Syrians and Libyans, who were just as unhappy as he about Arafat's slow-but-sure transition to a more 'moderate' position vis-à-vis Israel.

Khalaf's first move on being pushed out was to make a major tour of Eastern Europe, the Gulf Emirates, Kuwait, Tunisia and finally Libya. In five months he managed to collect 40 million dollars, now deposited in a private bank account in Europe, to finance actions independent of the Arafat and al-Wazir restrictions.

In February 1979 Khalaf had told a Lebanese crowd, 'Palestine cannot win until all the Arab sheikhs are deposed . . . the day is very close.' But on his fund-raising trip the Gulf sheikhs and emirs gave him large donations. Little of the money has gone towards fostering the Palestinian cause. Khalaf sent millions to the Kurds of Iraq to finance sabotage operations instigated by Libya and Syria against Iraqi objectives.

The Kurds get most of their Intelligence from Khalaf, who had also placed training facilities at the Kurds' disposal. He finances operations of the Lebanese Shia Amal organisation, a group devoted to subversive activities against the Turks; it was they who sabotaged a major oil pipeline in Turkey. Khalaf dislikes the Turks. All this would be 'normal' but it is in direct opposition to the orders of Arafat and al-Wazir who were doing their best to mediate the Iraqi-Iranian crisis, to shore up relations with Iraq, and to develop strong ties with Turkey. It is also in direct contravention of PLO policy which is, for the time, geared to breaking away from the Syrian-Libyan sphere of influence and alignment with the Iraqi camp to give the West the tactical impression of moderation.

Khalaf has pushed a wedge between Syria and Arafat, and is now considered both Syria's and Libya's man in the

PLO. He has played one PLO group against the other, correctly gauging that Arafat had pushed himself into a corner by attempting to court Western public opinion and thus angering the rejectionist Arab world.

Another sharp difference between Khalaf and the other two PLO leaders concerns his contacts with European terror groups representing both the right and the left. He has promised them every kind of material support, provided that they direct some of their activities against Israeli and Jewish objectives in Europe. There is reason to believe that the blast at the Bologna railway station early in 1980 was carried out with Khalaf's help. Foreign intelligence services believe that the railway station was not the selected target, but that the bomb was intended for a Jewish objective in the city.

Khalaf's name has been linked with both the Munich Oktoberfest massacre and the Paris synagogue bombing in 1980. He is known to be giving technical and financial assistance in West Germany to Karl Hoffman's fascists and to leftist groups such as the Baader-Meinhof gang, and is similarly involved with both the radical and the extreme right-wing terror movements in Italy.

Khalaf's strength within the Arab world derives not only from the support of the Syrians and the Libyans, but also from the personal information about his fellow-terrorists he has been able to amass during his years in power. He knows too much.

Arafat is worried by the threat from Khalaf, which is backed by the great wealth he has accumulated, and by extreme elements of the international terrorist brotherhood. Rank and file PLO members ask how long Arafat will be able to live with Khalaf working against him and against al-Wazir, and what will be the effect of this rivalry on the entire organisation. Should Arafat be killed or be forced out of power then Fatah, and with it the PLO, will change radically.

Arafat continues as chairman of the PLO simply because his is the best known name and his enemies concede that his international connections are unrivalled. Within the PLO he does not have the control he pretends to others that he has. For instance, in May 1980 he packed the PLO conference in Damascus in order to block a Fatah motion for the armed struggle 'to liquidate the Zionist entity politically, economically, militarily, culturally and ideologically.' He argued that this language was too strong for his new Western allies to accept. But he failed to stop the motion or to have it amended and it was carried.

Al-Wazir could probably not hold the movement on its present course—the gun and the olive branch approach. For all his talents as a military commander and an arch-terrorist he lacks both the political skill and the charisma for leadership of a large, complex group and would be unable to cope with the hold which Khalaf has developed. He hates the Syrians, for he believes that when they gaoled him in 1966—on suspicion of being behind a PLO plot to overthrow the government—they raided his apartment and murdered his two-year-old son by throwing him out of the fifth-floor window. Then they refused al-Wazir permission to attend the funeral. The antithesis of Khalaf, al-Wazir is a non-drinker and does not womanise. He is reputed to be incorruptible in the handling of the PLO's funds.

Arafat's relationship with the Syrians and the Libyans may be an ambiguous one, but at least it works when needed. Al-Wazir has none at all, and will probably never develop one. Moreover being in charge of operations on the West Bank, he is in constant contact with Jordan through the Joint Palestine-Jordan Commission and Jordan's representative on it, Hassan Ibrahim, the minister for the conquered territories. This contact with Jordan, the country which slaughtered thousands of Palestinians in the September 1970 purge, is condemned by almost the entire PLO hierarchy.

Even if Arafat stays, the unity of Fatah seems far from certain. The signs of discord are apparent. In October 1980, in Beirut, bullets ripped through the car of al-Wazir's confidant, Sa'id Sayel (Abu el-Walid) the commander of Fatah forces in Lebanon. He was slightly injured but his bodyguards were killed. Few doubt that Khalaf was behind the assassination attempt; what is more interesting is the reason for it.

Some days earlier Khalaf had complained that Sayel had informed the Kuwaitis that he, Khalaf, had masterminded an explosion in August 1980 which wrecked the offices of the Kuwait government official journal *Al-Rai Al-Aam*. At the time several Palestinians were arrested, and they told the Kuwaiti police that they were retaliating for restrictions that had recently been imposed on Palestinians in that country. But it was common knowledge around PLO headquarters that it was Khalaf who had carried out the attack to further embarrass Arafat, who only recently had to apologise to the Kuwaitis for the Palestinian hijacking of one of their airliners en route from Damascus.

There are sharp differences of opinion within the PLO command over the question of operations against Israel, over the form of action to be taken in Southern Lebanon, over whether the PLO should or should not mediate in the Iranian-Iraqi war and which side to support in the conflict. Until now, Arafat has managed to suppress internal differences by concentrating on the Zionist enemy. But inner conflict seems to have gone too far for suppression and mediation.

A recent incident has been interpreted by observers as the first shot in the power battle that will ultimately change the structure of the PLO. Khalaf's chief lieutenant, Morad Dajani (Abu Rajer), was arrested on charges of corruption and Arafat himself conducted the interrogation. Dajani was eventually released and supporters of Khalaf say that he suspects that Arafat fixed conditions for the release—and that they do not favour Khalaf. Mysterious assassinations were averaging one a week in 1981.

By 1981 Khalaf had gone too far to reconcile his differences with Arafat. He therefore secretly aligned himself with a small developing group in the PLO, Al-Thawra. This movement, whose name means The Revolution, came into being after President Sadat's visit to Jerusalem in 1977, in protest against the PLO's seeming impotence in dealing with the new reality. Al-Thawra's leaders, Taysir Hassan, Abdul Karim and Hamdi Abdul Said, are all loyal to Khalaf, who is their link to the Libyan purse.

Professor William Quandt of the University of Pennsylvania, in a detailed study,* divides the PLO membership into two political-religious groups. The majority are Sunni Muslims who are 'narrowly nationalistic in outlook.' Among these people 'Palestinian culture values seem to predispose individuals towards suspicion, competition, strong emotions and fluctuating loyalties in their political relationships,' Quandt says. Salah Khalaf and Walid al-Wazir fit this type. The other group is 'a significant minority' either not Palestinian by birth or not from the dominant Sunni population. These non-Sunni Palestinians 'tend to give priority to issues of radical and secular change.' George Habash, who is Greek Orthodox, and Nayef Hawatmeh, who is a Jordanian Christian, typify this group of radicals.

Western people, and especially those with policy-making responsibilities, need to understand the cultural, social, financial and political motivations of PLO leaders before making judgments on the viability and integrity of the PLO as a responsible political organisation. The West must also understand what the PLO and the 'Palestinian question' mean to the Arab world.

The European Council declaration in Venice, June 1980, is based on two false assumptions—that the Palestinian issue is the heart of the Arab-Israeli conflict and that a comprehensive peace settlement would produce an era of stability in the Middle East. Sadly, the Arab approach to the Palestinian question has been opportunistic rather than one of genuine concern. Between 1948-1967 Palestinian refugees languished in refugee camps ignored by the great mass of Arabs and unnoticed by the rest of the world. Only after Israel occupied the West Bank in 1967

* *The Politics of Palestinian Nationalism*, University of California Press, 1974.

did the Arabs show concern for the Palestinian people. The fundamental commitment of the Arabs is to the doctrine of pan-Arabism, not Palestinian self-determination. Arab animosity to Israel is the result of Israeli occupation of *Arab* land, not Palestinian land. Any solution to the Palestinian problem, short of Israel's removal from the Middle East, will only marginally affect Arab demands.

Major developments in the Middle East are not affected directly by the conflict; a comprehensive peace settlement would check neither the growth of the Muslim Brotherhood, nor solve the struggle between the Ba'athist Parties of Iraq and Syria. The potential of the Iranian revolution to destabilise the entire Arab world is independent of any outcome of the Arab-Israeli conflict. The traditional instability of the Middle East is rooted in the nature of inter-Arab rivalry.

The West cannot satisfy both Israel and the representative—self-appointed—of the Palestinian people, the PLO. Yet Western statesmen have chosen to walk a narrow path in an attempt to appease both sides without alienating the other. Unless either the PLO or Israel is prepared unconditionally to recognise the other the West cannot indefinitely support both sides simultaneously.

The PLO's aims are clear, either through public statement or overt act. These aims can be set down in this way:

• Rejection of UN Resolutions 242 and 338, which have provided a basis for peace negotiations in the Middle East, as well as all other proposals which may be designed to produce a negotiated settlement of the Arab-Israeli conflict.
• Rejection of the Camp David Agreements and in particular the treaty between Israel and Egypt—the only one of its kind in the Middle East.
• Affirmation of its intention to destroy the State of Israel by armed force. The PLO has broadly hinted that Jordan is next on the list, with other 'reactionary' states

in the area. This would mean Saudi Arabia, Oman, Kuwait and the Gulf emirates.

- Acclamation of the 'Islamic revolution' in Iran.
- Defence of the Soviet invasion of Afghanistan. The PLO was one of the few Arab and Muslim bodies to support the Soviet in its attempted take-over of a Muslim country.
- Creation of periodic chaos and bloodshed in Lebanon.
- General support for the aims of Colonel Gaddafi, the Libyan leader.
- Support of all kinds for international terrorism.
- Friendship with the Soviet Union and support by many PLO leaders for Marxist ideology though Communism is anathema to Islam.
- Declaration of hatred for the United States and for any countries of the Western Alliance which support US policies in the Middle East.

At a rally held in Beirut on June 16, 1980, three days after the European leaders made their Venice declaration of support for the Palestinians, Arafat said, 'Do not believe that it is possible to regain Palestine and to return to Jerusalem by means of a political statement. You will not return to Palestine or raise the flag of the revolution over Jerusalem other than by means of the rifle. We will not achieve political victory so long as we do not achieve military victory. You must strengthen the iron fist around the rifle which will lead to victory.'*

PLO spokesmen are generally frank and open about the organisation's tactics and intentions when they are speaking to Arab audiences or to Arab journalists. They are less direct when interviewed by Western journalists. But on June 29, 1981, Zehdi Terezi, the PLO 'ambassador' at the United Nations was as unequivocal as his chief.** 'We have not given up our struggle with the machine-gun, he said. 'It has to go along with our diplomatic offensive.'

* Quoted by *The Voice of Palestine*, Beirut, June 16, 1980
** In the BBC programme, *Panorama*.

Chapter Thirteen

The Vicious Circle

Late in 1981 it became clear that Black September, the deadly Palestinian "strike force", was being re-activated. The first signs of this appeared at Schwechat Airport, Vienna, where customs officials found arms in suitcases of two Palestinians. The men offered various explanations for the automatic weapons and hand grenades; one was that they had orders to attack a dissident faction of the PLO operating in Austria. The dissidents belong to a small terrorist group led by Sabri Khalil Bana (Abu Nidal). Advocating all-out war with Israel, the group was expelled from the PLO in 1974 because of its refusal to obey the leaders. Soon after this Abu Nidal claimed responsibility for the murder in Vienna of Heinz Nittel, a socialist politician and president of the Austro-Israel Society.

The two men arrested in August 1981 were members of a resurgent Black September and their probable target was President Sadat. Sadat had been in the United States and planned a stopover in Austria for a holiday at Schloss Klesheim and talks with Chancellor Kreisky. The plan was abruptly cancelled, after Austrian security officials notified Egypt of the Black September operation. Because of Austria's formal recognition of the PLO the incident embarrassed Chancellor Kreisky but the matter was speedily disposed of. After only an hour's trial one PLO man was sentenced to nine months' gaol—and the sentence was immediately suspended—while the judge accepted the plea of the other man that he had no idea of the contents of the bag he was carrying.

The Austrian incident was disturbing because only a week before, for the first time the Israeli Government and the PLO had come close to a formal agreement. They accepted a truce to end fighting in Lebanon. It was some slight evidence of trust and compromise on both sides. Arafat even pushed into line the Jibryl faction which did not want to obey the ceasefire. Austria and other nations applauded the PLO moderation.

Three days after the Vienna arrests, Muhammad Daoud Auda, a senior PLO official, was shot in a Warsaw café and seriously wounded. This Palestinian, better known as Abu Daoud, is accused of having participated in the killings of the Israeli athletes at the 1972 Munich Olympic Games and of two American diplomats in Khartoum in 1973. Polish Intelligence said that the shooting was planned by enemies of Abu Daoud within the PLO—though Daoud himself suggested that the attempted murder was the work of Mossad, a branch of the Israeli Intelligence Service.

The Black September plot and the Warsaw shooting show, once again, that the PLO has many faces and many factions. Those Western politicians who make a deal with Arafat could find that they have not necessarily made a deal with the PLO. In any case, a deal with one PLO chief does not usually bind the others. More dangerously, the PLO has a built-in booby trap for those world leaders who would negotiate with it. Not being democratically based, it uses words for only so long as they produce the results demanded. When words fail the gun and bomb come quickly into use. 'Talking with the PLO', in the democratic meaning of the phrase, can have no meaning until the Palestinians leave their weapons at home. Or until the Palestinian people renounce the PLO.

Intermittent attacks by PLO terrorists across the Lebanese border into Israel—by rocket or raiding party —and the continuing attacks on Israeli diplomats abroad goaded Israel to massive reprisals. When Israel's army crossed the border on June 13, 1982, the stated aim was to push the PLO back by 25 miles, thus making safe Israel's northern towns and kibbutzim. This incursion rapidly became a war to smash the PLO out of existence. The invading army split into three separate attacking columns. One headed west then north along the sea towards the PLO strongholds of Rashidiyah and Tyre. The central column rolled towards the PLO vantage point of Beaufort Castle, with the aim of pushing north along the Bekaa Valley. The third column opened an eastern front, intending to clear the PLO out of the 144 square mile zone of Lebanon known as 'Fatahland.'

The invasion, in military terms, was strikingly success-ful and many PLO men were either killed or captured. Finally, a hard core of fighters bottled up in West Beirut faced destruction unless they could escape by night or unless they accepted the Israeli offer of safe conduct to Syria along the road to Damascus.

Vast quantities of PLO war material, including sophisti-cated weapons systems, were captured. The Israelis were confident that they had broken the PLO's military power and this seemed beyond question. They had also put Israel beyond the physical reach of any form of PLO attack, since it could be assumed that neither Syria nor Jordan would permit raids from bases on their soil.

The PLO, though effectively removed from southern Lebanon, was not destroyed. Its funds were intact, it still had a strong leadership cadre and it could count on being re-armed by Warsaw Pack nations. Unable to strike directly into Israel, its leaders were planning, even as they were forced out of Lebanon, to revert to widespread terrorism outside the Middle East.

The Arab states made no move to help the PLO survive the most crushing blow ever to befall it. This is significant, for it shows that most Arab leaders would like to see the PLO destroyed; by 1982 it had become too menacing and too powerful to be tolerated. Unable to weaken the PLO themselves, the major Arab governments quietly wel-comed the Israeli action to smash the organisation. During the Israeli attack the major moral support for the PLO came from its friends in the West. Throughout the bitter days of violent fighting in the summer of 1982 the PLO was swearing bloody vengeance not only against Israel but against the 'uncaring' Arab world. It will at least have adequate weapons; just before the latest war Saudi Arabia granted a PLO delegation 250 million dollars to pay for new weapons from Soviet-bloc countries.

The Lebanese hoped that the Israel-PLO war would leave them free, after more than 12 years of torment, to re-establish their country as a sovereign state. Among ordinary Palestinians on the West Bank were faint stirrings of hope that they might be able to create a political entity free of PLO menace. If this happened, they believed, Israel would be much readier to permit a Palestinian state to be formed on the West Bank. Israeli leaders had always made clear that they would welcome Palestinian neighbours if they were not dominated by the PLO.

Even Syria, which had given so much help to the PLO, refused to give sanctuary to its rank-and-file terrorists on Syrian soil; the organisation had become too violent and too dangerous. And dangerous it remains. Arafat, Habash and others, interviewed during the 1982 war, showed that they had a fresh desire for vengeance.

The PLO would soon exploit new tactics against new targets with renewed terror, anywhere in the world.

TWO MINUTES OVER BAGHDAD
  by Amos Perlmutter, Michael Handel and Uri Bar-Joseph

"If the Iraqis get the bomb, it will be as though all the countries in this region are hanging from a light sewing thread, high above. Any attempt to use the bomb will lead immediately to the tearing of that thread . . ."
Raful Eitan, Israeli Chief-of-Staff

Early in 1980, the Israeli Government's worst fears—that an unstable Arab regime such as Iraq would acquire nuclear weapons—were realised. President Saddam Hussein had constructed a nuclear plant at Osirak, near Baghdad, and it was his declared intention to use the bomb against Israel . . .

Israeli Prime Minister Menachem Begin made an agonising decision—a flight of F-15 fighter aircraft and F-16 fighter-bombers, manned by perhaps the most skilled pilots in the world, would destroy the Iraqi nuclear plant. In TWO MINUTES OVER BAGHDAD, the true story of "Operation Babylon" is told for the first time.

SBN: 0 552 11939 3   Price: £1.75

A SELECTED LIST OF
FINE CORGI PAPERBACKS

While every effort is made to keep prices low, it is sometimes necessary to increase prices at short notice. Corgi Books reserve the right to show new retail prices on covers which may differ from those previously advertised in the text or elsewhere.

All these books are available at your book shop or newsagent, or can be ordered direct from the publisher. Just tick the titles you want and fill in the form below.

CORGI BOOKS, Cash Sales Department, P.O. Box 11, Falmouth, Cornwall.

Please send cheque or postal order, no currency.

Please allow cost of book(s) plus the following for postage and packing:

U.K. Customers—Allow 45p for the first book, 20p for the second book and 14p for each additional book ordered, to a maximum charge of £1.63.

B.F.P.O. and Eire—Allow 45p for the first book, 20p for the second book plus 14p per copy for the next 7 books, thereafter 8p per book.

Overseas Customers—Allow 75p for the first book and 21p per copy for each additional book.

NAME (Block Letters) _____

ADDRESS _____